Praise for the Book

Who Owns That Song? is a fascinating examination of the strange afterlife of one of our greatest poets. With formidable scholarship, A.R. Venkatachalapathy not only reveals how a motley group of film producers, politicians, movie stars and family members fought to seize control of Subramania Bharati's poems, but also sheds light on how literature shapes, and is shaped by, nationalism in modern India. Crisp, and wickedly alive to the ironies created when patriotism, greed and love of poetry battle one other, this slender book deeply enriches our understanding of Bharati's legacy.
Aravind Adiga, Man Booker winner for *The White Tiger*

This is a brilliant book by a superlative historian. With wit and verve, A.R. Venkatachalapathy traces the surprising story of how the state acquired the rights to Subramania Bharati's work and placed it in the public domain. *Who Owns That Song?* weaves together Bharati's biography, his work and the political history of twentieth-century India. Venkatachalapathy shows us how Bharati emerged as a vital force in the history of Indian nationalism and Tamil cultural revival, and he charts the battle over Bharati's legacy in the early years of independent India. This is essential reading: insightful and delightful in equal measure.
Sunil Amrith, MacArthur Prize Fellow

The ironies and ultimate triumph of Subramania Bharati's career, a towering figure of twentieth century Tamil culture, leap to life as never before in this sparkling, profound work of scholarly sleuthing and cultural criticism. Spooling back through the intriguing story of ownership over Bharati's writing, Venkatachalapathy brilliantly reconstructs the cultural milieu and ploys which transformed an indigent poet into a national cultural icon – his words freely woven into the popular imagination.
Sunil Khilnani, author of *The Idea of India*

Venkatachalapathy tells us, grippingly, how we – the people of India – have come to own the words of the master poet and writer Subramania Bharati. An intriguing story of literary vitality, nationalism and political will.
T.M. Krishna, musician, winner of the Magsaysay Award

I have often wondered how the light of A.R. Venkatachalapathy's historical scholarship focuses on the past, shines on the present and diffuses into the future. *Who Owns that Song?* possesses the same quality. By exploring the history of Subramania Bharati's copyright, this book enlightens us on the novel concept of nationalization of literary treasures, and rides us through the background, the nitty-gritty of the process and the various challenges that brought this to fruition. The racy narrative style makes for an interesting read. It is gratifying that a Tamil experience can be a lesson for world literature.
Perumal Murugan, author of *One Part Woman*

This page-turner of a book tells the extraordinary story of Bharati's tumultuous life, his failed attempts at publishing his poems and the posthumous battles over them among competing film producers, publishers and the state. A wonderfully rich study that raises many important questions over who owns poetry and who has the right to it.
Francesca Orsini, Chair, Centre for Literary, Cultural and Postcolonial Studies, SOAS

This slim volume is a little gem of Book History. The vigorously contested and unprecedented process through which the copyright of the great nationalist Tamil poet Subramania Bharati was 'nationalized', i.e. acquired by the state government, is here narrated in all its twists and turns. Such is the author's erudition and so engaging is his style that this book reads like a suspense novel by an omniscient narrator. It also raises vital issues of direct relevance to authorship, author-ity and the politics of ownership of art.
Harish Trivedi, former professor, University of Delhi

Who Owns That Song?

Subramania Bharati
Photograph taken in 1921, the last year of the poet's life.

Who Owns That Song?

The Battle for Subramania Bharati's Copyright

A.R. Venkatachalapathy

JUGGERNAUT BOOKS
C-I-128, First Floor, Sangam Vihar, Near Holi Chowk,
New Delhi 110080, India

First published in hardback by Juggernaut Books 2018
Published in paperback by Juggernaut Books 2024

Copyright © A.R. Venkatachalapathy 2018
English translation of Subramania Bharati's poems
copyright © M.L. Thangappa

10 9 8 7 6 5 4 3 2 1

The views and opinions expressed in this book are the author's own.
The facts contained herein were reported to be true as on the date
of publication by the author to the publishers of the book, and the
publishers are not in any way liable for their accuracy or veracity.

All rights reserved. No part of this publication may be reproduced,
transmitted, or stored in a retrieval system in any form or by any means
without the written permission of the publisher.

P-ISBN: 9789353458669
E-ISBN: 9789353455699

Typeset in Adobe Caslon Pro by R. Ajith Kumar, Noida

Printed at Thomson Press India Ltd

for Professor V.K. Natraj

Subramania Bharati is planning to publish all his manuscripts ... in forty volumes in print runs of 10,000 copies each. There is little doubt that these four lakh copies will get sold out in Tamilnadu as easily and as quickly as kerosene and matchboxes.

– from Bharati's prospectus for his publication programme, 1920

Is it right ... to permit the immortal poet of Tamilnadu to be locked up in an iron safe and be made a matter of business?
... We have every right to ask the people living in a free country, 'Who owns Bharati?'
Why shouldn't the Madras government proclaim that 'Bharati's poems and writings are the property of Tamilnadu. No individual has any right over it.'

– from a pamphlet, February 1948

For some years now, the people in Tamilnadu – the literate and the illiterate, the Congressman and the Communist – have joined in a campaign against me for the sin of possessing the copyright in poet's works ... The question of nationalisation of the works of a poet or author is raised in no other part of India. Do not people consider it quite natural that the works of Tagore or Sarojini Devi ... [are] published by the author or his or her heirs, legal representatives, assigns or the publishers to whom the works might have been sold?

– C. Visvanathan, Bharati's half-brother and publisher (1949)

There is a popular feeling that the works of Sri C. Subramania Bharati, the great Tamil poet of Modern Tamil Renaissance, should be acquired by the Government and made available for the use of the public generally at as cheap a cost as possible.

– T.S. Avinashilingam Chettiar, Education Minister, on the floor of Madras Legislative Assembly, 12 March 1949

Bharatiar's works were held as private property and ... nobody could use them for any purpose without the permission of those individual owners. Therefore, in order to make them public property, the Government purchased the entire right of publishing Bharatiar's works ... The Government has decided to release the entire right to the public ... Bharatiar's poetical works imprisoned in the hands of private individuals and subsequently within the four walls of the Secretariat will hereafter be completely released and will have complete freedom.

– C. Subramaniam, Law, Education and Finance Minister, on the floor of Madras Legislative Assembly, 14 March 1955

Dramatis Personae

Subramania Bharati. Unsung poet, neglected in his life, attains posthumous fame, with his books remaining bestsellers till date.

Chellamma. The poet's widow, endures dire poverty after marriage to her eccentric husband, but does not get a penny when his works become a posthumous commercial success.

C. Visvanathan. The poet's half-brother, buys the copyright when the works have little commercial value. The object of envy and popular agitation when he reaps unexpected windfalls, and later forced to give up his copyright at distress price.

Jeshinglal K. Mehta. Gujarati businessman who invests in a poet despite being unable to read Tamil.

AV. Meiyappan. Movie mogul and businessman. Makes a calculated investment at the right moment by buying the broadcast rights of the poet's writings. Files a suit for infringement of these rights and has to face adverse public opinion.

T.K. Shanmugam. Idealistic actor who enters the theatre at the age of six, works with the father of the Tamil stage and will not brook a businessman's stranglehold over his favourite poet's songs.

Dramatis Personae

P. Jeevanandam. Communist agitator who can stir public emotion through his selfless work and fiery speeches. An ardent admirer of the poet's works, he takes them to the masses.

Omandur P. Ramaswamy Reddiar. Rustic Gandhian who, as head of the Madras government, is faced with the unenviable task of balancing popular demand with a private (intellectual) property issue.

T.S. Avinashilingam Chettiar. Man of impeccable honesty and administrative skills; as education minister, he must achieve Bharati's nationalization, cutting through the morass of legal issues and public opinion.

Contents

	Prologue	xv
1.	The Making of a Poet	1
2.	The Afterlife of a Master Spirit	29
3.	Make it Public!	55
4.	Nationalization and After	115
	Epilogue	165
	A Note on the Sources	170
	A Note on the Worth of Money	177
	Selected Poems of Subramania Bharati	179
	Acknowledgements	189
	Other Books by the Author	192

Prologue

Copyright Claws

Copyright is a term that occurs only once in the writings of Subramania Bharati, and he would not have recognized the © symbol that figures in the imprint pages of every published book today. Bharati is not known to have listened to gramophone recordings, or sound recordings of any form, or ever stepped into a cinema hall. He would have been amazed to learn that poems could earn money by being used in these new media. A poet who died in poverty – with half his works uncollected or unpublished in his lifetime – he could not have imagined that his copyright would be the subject of legal wrangles, with film-makers and publishers vying to acquire it. He would undoubtedly have been pleased to know that the Tamil public at large appreciated his work, at least posthumously, and demanded that his works be made public property, free of copyright.

On 12 March 1949, when the education minister of Madras announced, 'There is popular feeling that the works of ... C. Subramania Bharati, the great Tamil poet of Modern Tamil Renaissance, should be acquired by the Government and made available for the use of the public generally at as cheap a cost as possible,' it inaugurated a unique moment in the global history of copyright.

When five years later the minister's successor declared in the Legislative Assembly that 'the Government are proposing to ... immediately releas[e] the entire right to the public so much so Bharatiar's poetical works imprisoned in the hands of private individuals and subsequently within the four walls of the Secretariat will hereafter be completely released and will have complete freedom', a revolution in that literary history was complete.

This was the first time ever, anywhere in the world, that the state acquired the copyright of a writer and put all his writings in the public domain. Since then no public figure – not Tagore, not Gandhi, not Nehru, not even Ambedkar – has had the honour of their works freed from the claws of copyright before the lapse of the stipulated time period. To comprehend this, an understanding of the meaning and basic legal features of copyright is essential.

Prologue

Copyright, simply put, is the right to own and make copies of a work of original expression. This right is vested in its creator and is internationally recognized, subject to relevant national laws. 'Original work' includes the efforts of a writer, composer, painter, or other such creative artist (although, in this book, we will be concerned only with the work of a writer). Copyright also includes 'subsidiary rights' such as broadcast rights, film rights, dramatization rights, performance rights and translation rights.

Although it is a property right, it is qualified by the fact that the purpose of creating a work is to disseminate it. In recent decades, with the acceleration of globalization, it has come to be clubbed with what are called intellectual property rights, or IPR, which include patents, trademarks, etc. As a property right, copyright can be traded, sold, assigned or bequeathed. The various subsidiary rights can also be disentangled and handled separately. The creator usually authorizes a publisher to print multiple copies of his/her works and in return gets a share of the revenue, termed as royalty. Making unauthorized copies of the work amounts to copyright infringement. Exceptions to this come under the 'fair use' doctrine that permits limited use for purposes of education, reporting, criticism, parody, etc. Infringement is usually a civil, and not a criminal, matter.

In addition, there are moral rights – the right to

attribution and the preservation of the integrity of the work without mutilation or distortion – which cannot be alienated even by the author.

Copyright was born in late seventeenth-century England with the advent of print technology and the possibility of making identical copies in large numbers. Central to its emergence was the commodification of the work of art, and its commercial value in the market. With the mushrooming of ever newer forms of reproduction, the ambit of copyright continues to expand, and consequently has proved to be contentious.

The copyright of the creator over his/her work, when not sold or licensed to another, is passed on to the heir. It lapses only after a certain period of time following his/her death. According to present Indian copyright laws, it expires sixty years after the author's death. It is then that the work passes into the public domain for free and unrestricted use. This provision strikes a balance between protecting the creator's rights and the benefit afforded by the work to the public.

By acquiring the copyright of Bharati, the government of Madras short-circuited this process and put Bharati's works in the public domain a quarter of a century before January 1972, when, in the normal course of law in force at that time, the copyright would have lapsed. Rather than being a violation of a legal right, this action of the state was intended as an unprecedented honour to the author.

~

As mentioned, the word copyright barely occurs in Bharati's writings. It does not figure in the title pages of his books published in his lifetime, and in any case imprint pages were non-existent then. Subsidiary rights would have been unknown to him. If someone translated him into another language, he would have considered it an honour rather than as an infringement of his copyright. In fact, when the Irish poet James H. Cousins, evidently without prior express permission, translated him into English, Bharati advertised it proudly. Despite the fact that one of his books was published in South Africa, Bharati was innocent of terms such as 'territorial rights' – the right to authorize copies of a work for different geographical regions.

There is no proof of Bharati having listened to any sound recordings despite the gramophone having entered India by the time of his death. Talkies were only born in the Tamil cultural world ten years after his death, but there is no evidence of him having watched any silent films either, even though he could have easily done so if he had walked a mile from his office or from his home.

Bharati may be excused for giving these new media a miss; after all, he had a tough enough time trying to make a living through writing, let alone pondering the potentialities of these budding forms of communication.

It is a sad irony that the works of such a man should trigger copyright tussles (involving Bharati's family, the eventual copyright holders, and the state) within a decade of his death.

How did Subramania Bharati, a man who died prematurely, in obscurity and impoverished, come to achieve this status and receive the posthumous honour of his copyright being nationalized?* What were the social impulses and cultural forces that fuelled the campaign demanding Bharati's works be made public property? Can the copyright of a cultural icon be defined narrowly as property? What rights do family members have over an author's work after giving up their rights? What are the implications of someone unrelated to the artist's family acquiring copyright of a cultural icon? Who speaks for the moral rights of a cultural icon posthumously? What

---

* Nationalization usually refers to the takeover of ownership, with or without compensation, of a major firm or industry by the state. Contemporary activists who demanded that the Madras government acquire the copyright of Bharati's works and make it available for free public use employed this term – in English and in Tamil translation – and I therefore employ it to refer to this process.

claim does the larger society have over his texts? What are the implications for the scholarly study of his texts in the public domain?

These are some of the questions thrown up by the drama that led to the nationalization of Subramania Bharati's works. To understand these questions, and to begin to answer them, we need to travel 135 years back in time to India's southern corner, Ettayapuram.

1
The Making of a Poet

Ettayapuram

A small town in southern Tamilnadu, Ettayapuram seems an unlikely place for the birth of the greatest modern Tamil poet. Bereft of rivers, in the rain shadow of both the south-west and north-east monsoons, it is home only to wild streams carrying flash floods. The perennial Tamiraparani skirts this arid region and marks it out ecologically and culturally from the wet zone. Scarcely mentioned in early historical narratives, this region came under the plough only with the advent of Telugu-speaking agricultural castes from the north in the late sixteenth century.

But a spell or two of rain could turn its black soil bountiful, yielding a rich harvest of millets, pulses and groundnut. Well suited to growing cotton, a new variety of cotton called 'tinnies' (after Tinnevelly or Tirunelveli, the erstwhile composite district in which it was located), flourished there in the mid-nineteenth century and was the cornerstone of an economic upswing.

During the pacification of the southern countryside in the late eighteenth century, the rulers of Ettayapuram were a steadfast ally of the British East India Company. In 1803, Ettayapuram became a zamin under the new revenue settlement, and was the second most populous of the zamindaris in the Madras Presidency and the third largest in terms of acreage and income.

When the American Civil War broke out in 1860, disrupting cotton supply from the American South, it resulted in a cotton boom. As the locals say, 'The scorpion stung the coconut tree but the poison shot through the palm tree.' Cotton carding, ginning and spinning mills mushroomed, effecting major economic and social transformations. The Ettayapuram zamin accounted for about half the cotton production in the region.

Though from an impoverished family, Bharati's father, S. Chinnaswamy Iyer, demonstrated sufficient skills to find employment in the zamin and won the zamindar's confidence. Soon he found himself a bride, Lakshmi, the daughter of the local munsif. Bharati was born to this couple on 11 December 1882 and named

Subramanian. When he was five, Subbiah, as he was fondly called at home, lost his mother, and he was raised by his maternal grandmother. His father remarried two years later. By all accounts, Bharati's stepmother was exceptional, showering love on the young boy.

Bharati's father was a disciplinarian, and he did not permit the boy to indulge in childhood sports. A loner, Bharati kept to his books. He also promptly fell in love with a girl. Though conservative Bharati aficionados dismiss it as calf love, that is not how he would describe it in his autobiography. The precocious Bharati began to compose verses at a young age. In a barely fictionalized autobiography, *Chinna Sankaran Kathai* (The Story of Little Sankaran), written when Bharati was thirty-one, he would satirize the pedantic nature of the poetry he wrote as a boy. At the age of eleven he was conferred the title 'Bharati' (the Hindu goddess of learning) in the Ettayapuram court. Bharati was a rather common suffix that poets adopted in the eighteenth and nineteenth centuries. There were scores of Bharatis before Subramania Bharati but they were eclipsed by our bard who became *the* Bharati.

Though Chinnaswamy Iyer was not encouraging of his son's literary pursuits, he thought highly enough of Bharati's talents to feel that the high school in Ettayapuram was not good enough for him. Iyer sent him off to Hindu High School in the nearby town of Tirunelveli when Bharati was thirteen, and he studied there for three years. In 1897, at the age of fifteen, he was married – a child marriage that Bharati did not approve of but could not protest.

Chinnaswamy Iyer was a resourceful man, and in 1892 he launched a cotton ginning factory. He managed to raise enough capital, including a tidy sum from the zamindar, but the company collapsed within a few years. Later, Bharati would blame the British for conspiring to wreck this indigenous enterprise. The collapse ruined Chinnaswamy Iyer, and probably led to his premature death when Bharati was only sixteen.

'Why was I born in this wretched country!' he lamented in his autobiography. His maternal grandmother became his guardian and Bharati was sent to Varanasi where his aunt lived with her husband. The couple, who managed a charitable inn at Hanuman Ghat for pilgrims from the Tamil country, was especially fond of Bharati.

The Radical

Bharati arrived in the sacred Hindu city sometime in late 1898, a few months after his father's death. Fin-de-siècle Varanasi was an exciting place bursting with literary activity and cultural politics, and the first whiffs of radicalism touched Bharati. Its immediate impact was on his coiffure and sartorial style. Bharati cut off his traditional tuft, cropped his hair (like a Bengali, it was said), shaved off his beard, and began to sport what became the iconic twirled moustache, scandalizing family and community – Tamil Brahmins then did not usually sport moustaches. He also took to wearing a turban and a dark coat with a white cravat of sorts. Bharati cleared the entrance examination of Allahabad University but little else is known of his academic life. He most certainly learned Hindi, and brushed up his already good Sanskrit and English.

Like many in his generation, Bharati was 'crushed by English poetry'. He was influenced by the Romantic poets but the radical Shelley, rather than Wordsworth, was his favourite. He adopted the nom de plume of Shelley-dasan (disciple of Shelley), organized a Shellyean guild and, briefly, even turned atheist.

Events took an interesting turn when the Ettayapuram zamindar attended the Delhi Durbar to celebrate the accession of King Edward VII to the Emperor of India. He stopped at Varanasi on the way and asked Bharati to return to the zamin. Bharati obliged, probably returning in February 1903. His primary job was to be a companion and court poet to the zamindar. But Bharati was not cut out to be a hanger-on. After a year and a half, he quit the Ettayapuram zamin, with a biting poem criticizing the goings-on at court as his parting shot. Bharati mercilessly satirized the zamindar in the incomplete but hilarious *Chinna Sankaran Kathai*.

Meanwhile, in July 1904, his first poem appeared in print in *Viveka Bhanu*, a scholarly monthly published from Madurai. Titled '*Thanimai Irakkam*' (Solitude) – a typical Romantic theme – it is a sonnet, a prosodic form then new to Tamil. In August 1904 he served as a replacement teacher in a Madurai school for a hundred days – the only time in his life when he depended on an activity other than writing for sustenance.

Introduction to Nationalism

In November 1904 Bharati caught G. Subramania Iyer's eye. Subramania Iyer, the doyen of Indian journalism, was the founder of the nationalist daily *The Hindu*, and later launched the first Tamil daily, *Swadesamitran*. An early nationalist, he was one of the most important advocates of economic nationalism. Unlike many of his colleagues, he held strong social reform views, conducting the remarriage of his widowed daughter in the face of tough opposition.

Bharati's entry into the world of journalism, as subeditor of *Swadesamitran*, coincided with an important moment in the rise of Indian nationalism. As he once remarked, 'In the year *Subhakrithu* [1902–03] was born the new path called "patriotism" that is the source of all that is good.' Viceroy Curzon, in an effort to weaken the nationalist movement with its epicentre in Bengal, proposed to partition the admittedly straggling province, but on communal lines – a Hindu west and a Muslim east. The partition had the opposite effect, triggering the rise of the Swadeshi Movement.

In the annual session at Calcutta in December 1906, the Congress adopted a programme of Swadeshi – indigenous enterprise, boycott of foreign goods and national education. This inaugurated the moment of mass nationalist mobilization in India. Until then, nationalist activity meant conducting hall meetings, making speeches in English and passing pious resolutions which were forwarded to the British masters. The Swadeshi Movement brought nationalism to the streets. Bengal was agog with political activity, and Punjab and Bombay also became new centres of political movement.

Madras, until then derided as 'the benighted province', soon joined the Swadeshi front line. An extraordinary Swadeshi effort was afoot not only in the city of Chennai but also in the far southern corner of the country. If in other parts of the country Swadeshi meant making candles and bangles, in the coastal town of Tuticorin, freedom fighter V.O. Chidambaram Pillai spectacularly launched the Swadeshi Steam Navigation Company, the earliest indigenous shipping venture.

Bharati, all of twenty-two, was in the thick of events. As he cut his journalistic teeth, he kept pace with news of the nationalist movement across the country, and was boned up on the happenings in Bengal. Soon he was also editing *Chakravartini*, 'a Tamil monthly devoted mainly to the elevation of Indian ladies'.

July 1906 saw the arrival of Swami Abhedananda – a direct disciple of Ramakrishna and a lieutenant of Vivekananda – in Chennai. With its focus on cultural nationalism and national resurgence, Vivekananda's message had a particular appeal for Bharati. On a visit to Calcutta to attend the Congress session later that year, Bharati met another of Vivekananda's disciples, Sister Nivedita – an Irish woman, born Margaret Noble. The meeting had a deep impact on Bharati. Nivedita asked him why his wife had not accompanied him. If half the nation was enslaved, how could the other half hope to win freedom, she asked an embarrassed Bharati. More dramatically, if apocryphally, she is said to have torn her robe, pointed to her skin and asserted that unless Indians developed a hatred for white skin, India had little hope of liberation. Bharati would go on to dedicate three of his first publications to her, referring to her as 'Gurumani', his guru and teacher.

The Making of a Poet

During the same time that Bharati experienced these transformational encounters, the Congress witnessed a rift. While the moderates led by Gopal Krishna Gokhale wanted to follow constitutional methods, the new brand of nationalists – the so-called extremists that included Bal Gangadhar Tilak, Aurobindo Ghose, Lala Lajpat Rai and Bipin Chandra Pal – ridiculed their mendicancy and advocated aggressive methods of agitation involving the masses. Some of them even toyed with violent methods. On this issue, the politics of G. Subramania Iyer appeared ambivalent, leaving his young protégé dissatisfied. So when the new Tamil weekly *India* was launched, Bharati eagerly took up its de facto editorship and made it the mouthpiece of the extremists. He critically chronicled the Swadeshi Movement and was all fire in his attack on the colonial government. Bharati was the earliest to introduce a racy style in Tamil political journalism and also the first to publish political cartoons.

Around this time, he began to write songs with patriotic content and nationalist fervour. These songs demonstrate the distance he had travelled since 1897 when he wrote a long verse epistle to the zamindar of Ettayapuram – from a pedantic style bristling with tough conjugations to a more direct style with great emotive appeal. Often employing popular tunes from older songs, he filled them with new content for a larger and more inclusive public. The songs dealt with the glory of the motherland and its current fallen state, colonial exploitation, eulogies of nationalist leaders, and ridicule of moderate leaders and their mendicant ways.

Bharati also composed two long poems aimed at stirring up nationalist passion, adapted from the clarion calls of Shivaji and Guru Gobind Singh to their followers. Bharati was one of the first to write such exhortatory poems in Tamil, and these became powerful ammunition in the nationalist arsenal through the decades leading up to independence. More than a century later, lines and phrases from these poems have passed into common language, and many of them will live as long as a quest for freedom remains.

'Poetry, working for the cause of the nation, and never to be idle even for a moment, is my occupation,' wrote Bharati in one of his famous poems, *Vinayakar Nanmani Malai*. But poetry was not just his occupation; it was his vocation, his calling and his very life. That he made little money in this occupation and spent much of his life in straitened circumstances is another matter.

Bharati was an author, poet and journalist his entire life. Of the twenty books published during his lifetime, only four saw reprints, each fewer than a thousand copies. The price of his publications ranged from zero – his first work was distributed free of cost – to one rupee, the price of his last book. His books of poems, on which his reputation and fame rest, were sold for a couple of annas each. Most of his early works were self-published; his later books were published by an admirer of his.

Bharati's first publication happened through a patron in late 1907: three of his poems were collected in a four-page booklet financed by a leading moderate leader of Madras. In early 1908 Bharati published three books: *Swadesa Geethangal* (Nationalist Songs), a Tamil translation of Tilak's *Tenets of the New Party* and a booklet on the Madras extremists' trip to the Surat Congress.

The year 1907 was particularly hectic. Bharati organized and participated in many public meetings, a high point being Bipin Chandra Pal's visit to Chennai and his week-long lectures on the sands of Marina Beach that drew thousands of listeners. Bharati played a key role in organizing a delegation to the annual Congress session in Surat in December 1907. Meanwhile, the crisis in the Congress party was heading for a showdown, leading to the infamous event where the moderates and extremists came to blows, and the Congress suffered a split. However, this gave Bharati the opportunity to meet Tilak, Aurobindo and other stalwarts of the Swadeshi Movement, and he returned to Chennai all fired up.

The Swadeshi Movement peaked in the following months. In Tuticorin, Chidambaram Pillai's shipping venture posed a serious challenge to the British monopoly and he further infuriated the government by leading a strike in the British-owned cotton mills. Chidambaram Pillai was arrested and sentenced to two life terms of imprisonment. A wave of repression swept through the country. Subramania Iyer was arrested despite his old age and his leprosy. Tilak was deported to Burma.

The government was seriously considering prosecuting Bharati for his public speeches and his writings in *India* were being watched. Bharati got wind of the government's design through a tip-off.

Pondicherry, some 150 km from Chennai, was then a French enclave. Civil debtors and, occasionally, petty criminals and book pirates sought refuge in French India to escape police action. In an inspired move, Bharati escaped the enclosing police dragnet, and arrived in Pondicherry in August 1908. Taking a cue from Bharati, Aurobindo and V.V.S. Aiyar would also seek political refuge in Pondicherry. Meanwhile, the de jure editor of *India* was prosecuted and sentenced to five years of rigorous imprisonment for what were essentially Bharati's crimes – the one blemish in the poet's life.

India was revived within weeks of Bharati's move to Pondicherry, and a new daily, *Vijaya*, was also launched. He also began to edit *Karmayogi*, a Tamil monthly modelled on Aurobindo's English monthly of the same name. Bharati was back with a vengeance. As the Morley–Minto reforms were rolled out, unleashing the genie of Muslim communalism through the introduction of separate electorates, Bharati's attacks on the colonial government became more strident. Idealistic youth carried out a spate of bomb attacks, and he squarely blamed the government for triggering such desperate acts.

The government passed the draconian Indian Press Act in 1910 to silence the press. Bharati prefaced an essay on sculpture and poetry written at that time with: 'If we write on this subject the new press act will not touch us. Let's at least enlighten our readers on this subject!' Sarcasm could not stop the inevitable. The entry of *India* and *Vijaya* into British Indian territory was prohibited, and the journals immediately wound up. Bharati bid goodbye to the readers, stating that if the government did not believe in lawful dissent, nationalists would have to seek other means to continue their resistance.

To add to his troubles, in June 1911 the collector of Tirunelveli, Robert Ashe, was shot dead at Maniyachi railway station. This would be the only political assassination in the Tamil country during the freedom struggle. Two pamphlets calling for an armed insurrection against the British were circulated in the region before the assassination. Some of those arrested in connection with the murder had in their possession Bharati's books and journals. The British suspected Bharati's hand in the drafting of the pamphlets, even though no conclusive proof has emerged to prove his involvement till date.

A warrant was issued and a reward placed on Bharati's head. Police surveillance, already oppressive, became worse, and Pondicherry was crawling with British Indian secret police, spies and paid informers. Even a kidnapping was planned. Mails were routinely intercepted and money remittances confiscated.

What sustained Bharati amidst this turmoil was the intellectual camaraderie with Aurobindo, until Aurobindo cocooned himself in spiritual exercises, and with V.V.S. Aiyar, who was deeply invested in both classical and modern literature. Bharati's personality also attracted a bevy of bright young men who sustained his intellectual production.

During this period (1909–10), Bharati published four books: two of poetry and two of fiction. Of these, *Kanavu*, his autobiography in verse, and *Aariloru Pangu*, a social reform novelette, were proscribed by the Madras government on grounds of sedition.

The Poet and His Vocation

Bharati hadn't even turned thirty then. Though primarily a writer, his years in Chennai during the heady days of the Swadeshi Movement had been dominated by politics and journalism. In 1913 his friend Subramania Siva launched the monthly review *Jnanabhanu* that gave Bharati some scope for publishing his writings. Two years later Bharati found a regular avenue for publication in *Swadesamitran*. Though the magazine prohibited him from writing about politics, he provided sustained commentary on happenings in India and the world. Despite being a Tamil writer, he occasionally wrote in English. He often expressed his political views in the correspondence columns of *The Hindu*. He contributed short essays in Annie Besant's *New India* and *Commonweal*, and in Aurobindo's *Arya*. Writing in 1914, Bharati recalled, 'After I came to Pondicherry, I was living as an independent journalist not attached to any particular paper but receiving money from various newspapers for signed articles.'

In Pondicherry he had begun sustained poetical writing. With few political distractions, by 1912, at the age of thirty, he emerged as a prodigious poet. During these years, Bharati wrote two of his three great poetical works: *Panchali Sabatham* and *Kuyil*, the third being *Kannan Pattu*. *Panchali Sabatham*, a long poem of 415 verses, begins with Duryodhana scheming to draw the Pandavas into a game of dice and ends dramatically with Draupadi's vow. Though the narrative and its details closely follow the Mahabharata, the chunk of the story Bharati chose to rewrite leaves little doubt about his intent. It is impossible not to read it as an allegory of the freedom struggle. The dilemmas of the nationalist movement find their echo in each unforgettable line. The poem ends with Draupadi taking the earth-shaking vow not to tie her hair until it has been washed with Kaurava blood. The plight of Mother India under her colonial masters comes readily to mind.

Kuyil is in a completely different register. This poem of 744 lines is a fantasy. The narrator-poet falls hopelessly in love with a kuyil (koel) and its mesmerizing voice. However, she jilts him, first for a monkey and then a bull. When the narrator kills her, the kuyil transforms into a beautiful damsel and tells him about a curse from a previous birth when the two had been lovers. The poem ends with the realization that it is all a dream but not before Bharati teases would-be critics with the possibility of reading it as a Vedantic allegory. Since then there have been various studies with precisely the reading that Bharati foresaw. Such readings notwithstanding, the poem bristles with humour and is full of lines of sheer poetic genius and some of the most memorable words on love ever written in Tamil. The voice of the kuyil, for instance, is described as *minnal suvai* – the taste of lightning.

By this time, Bharati had begun to write poems on Kannan, the dark god Krishna, addressing him as the beloved, lover, king, guru, disciple, father, mother, son, girl child, lord, favourite deity, servant and friend. Predictably, the best poems are those of Kannan as beloved and lover. They draw on the rich medieval Tamil poetry of the Alwars, the progenitors of the Bhakti movement for whom the transcendental god is reached through passionate and unqualified devotion. Bharati later collected these poems as *Kannan Pattu*.

The publication of the first part of *Panchali Sabatham* in 1912 was followed the next year by *Puthiya Aathichudi*, a didactic poem, and the year after by *Matha Manivachagam*, a collection of his patriotic poems, and *The Fox with the Golden Tail*, a satire exposing Annie Besant and mocking the Theosophical Movement as 'the most colossal spiritual fraud of the ages'. Except for *Matha Manivachagam*, which was published in South Africa, all his books thus far were self-published. From 1917 a close associate and admirer of Bharati began to publish him. In this way, the artisanal stage in Bharati's career as a publisher-writer came to an end.

With this came a change in Bharati's understanding of book publishing. In the preface to his autobiographical poem *Kanavu* (1910), he wrote, 'That the printing of this book is not good is not my fault. It is the fault of the rich men of our country,' squarely blaming the shoddy production standards of his books on an absence of patronage. Two years later, the dedication of *Panchali Sabatham* read: 'To those gifted poets who are going to write epics which will give undying life and light to the Tamil language, and to those patrons who are going to aid them in the appropriate fashion, this book is dedicated.'

Counterposing this lingering faith in patronage there appears an important shift in his perception of the audience. In the preface to *Kanavu*, he remarked: 'This little book of verse is written in a novel way ... Its nature lies in the first person: that is, the hero narrates his story himself; that's the style adopted ... I am publishing this little book to see if this is acceptable to the learned men of Tamil. If these learned men test it and approve it, I will publish more of this sort.' Read alongside the preface to *Panchali Sabatham*, the shift seems dramatic: 'Simple words; a simple style; an easily grasped rhythm; a lilt liked by the common people – anyone who writes an epic with these qualities today will actually give new life to our mother tongue. Not only must it be easily comprehensible to all Tamil people familiar with books, even if their reading habit spans only a couple of years, but must also not fall short of artistic requirements.' From placing his faith in the 'learned men' of an earlier generation, Bharati now cast his lot with the emerging class of neoliterate readers. Thus, during this period,

The Making of a Poet

Bharati's attitude towards patronage and the reading public was marked by ambivalence.

A few years later, in 1916, he wrote a few articles on book publishing in general. They are insightful essays on the course that book publishing had taken in Tamilnadu. His views on patronage had by then undergone a clear change.

> The world over, the custom of practising various arts with the support of kings and lords has long gone. We must now begin relying on the people. From now on support and succour for the arts will come from the common people. It is the duty of artists to instil good taste in them. It will yield them good returns. A lord may at best give [artists] Rs 100 a month. But if people get together and contribute a quarter of a rupee each, they will get a thousand rupees a month. We must make the people our masters.
>
> The country is king. If you instil this king with some knowledge, the arts will never suffer.

Bharati's notebooks of the time contain lists of topics he wanted to write on that reveal his immersion in the creative process. His prose too was no pushover but is highly underestimated by critics and readers alike.

Although his stories, numbering about sixty, of varying length and running into many hundreds of pages, did not achieve the form of either the short story or the novel, they demonstrate his success in fashioning lively modern prose. *Chinna Sankaran Kathai*, one of the earliest life-writings in Tamil, remains an exemplar of self-deprecating humour. A temperamental poet, Bharati relied on inspiration. Likening poesy to a whimsical lover, he took issue with her for frequently abandoning him. His poems were often the result of short bursts of poetic intensity. Sometime during his exile in Pondicherry, inspired by Vedic hymns and Walt Whitman, he experimented with prose poems and was the first to do so in Tamil, and possibly in any Indian language. He was also knowledgeable about haiku, the Japanese poetic form.

The End

Bharati's diary jottings also speak of his confusion, his dire financial condition and his creativity being affected by worldly needs and poverty. A long spell of illness that afflicted his younger daughter left him shattered. At this time he took to tobacco and opium. A man of an already spiritual bent of mind with interest in Shakta rituals, Bharati cultivated relationships with wandering fakirs, some of whom he took to be his spiritual preceptors. Such relationships and practices complicated his eccentricities.

World War I put further pressure on his politics. With Britain and France on the same side of the war, his political exile was proving to be difficult. Being in Pondicherry further cut him off from the political events in mainland India.

As his exile extended interminably, Pondicherry was becoming claustrophobic. Bharati yearned for fresh air. His repeated pleas to the Madras government regarding its stance on his political status elicited only routine replies. In a fit of desperation, he had even written a long open letter to Ramsay MacDonald, the labour leader and future prime minister of Britain, 'on police rule in India' but to no avail.

By the end of the war, Bharati was a demoralized man. Barely a week after the signing of the armistice on 11 November 1918, Bharati stepped out of Pondicherry and was promptly arrested. On making a formal declaration to renounce politics, and agreeing to pre-censorship by the police for a period, he was released after three weeks in jail. Having been in exile for over a decade, Bharati had no place to call home. He repaired to his father-in-law's in Kadayam. If he was not made to feel particularly welcome there, it is but understandable.

A year earlier, Bharati began to be published by his young friend and admirer Parali S. Nellaiyappa Pillai, the only publisher to publish his poems in his lifetime. When he was still a young man, Nellaiyappa Pillai became politicized and took an active part in Swadeshi activities from 1907 onwards. In 1909 he went to Pondicherry and began to work in the Swadeshi papers there and forged a close relationship with Bharati, becoming a lifelong admirer. On Bharati's return to Chennai in 1913, Nellaiyappa Pillai was instrumental in placing his writings in the Chennai press. Nellaiyappa Pillai also worked for various nationalist journals and frequently reproduced the scattered and unpublished writings of Bharati. He continued to publish many essays in the poet's memory after Bharati died.

In the final years of Bharati's life, Nellaiyappa Pillai took it upon himself to publish Bharati's writings, even with the limited means at his disposal. What the two men shared was not a simple author–publisher relationship. All three of Bharati's surviving letters to him speak of publishing matters, yet absent from these is a single word about contract, royalty or rights. Nellaiyappa Pillai considered it his god-given duty, rather than a matter of business, to publish Bharati's books. As the only publisher of Bharati's poems in his lifetime, his name would figure prominently in the battle for Bharati's copyright.

The poems *Kannan Pattu*, *Nattu Pattu*, *Pappa Pattu* and *Murasu* were all published in 1917. Nellaiyappa Pillai's poignant publisher's notes show he was performing what he thought was his duty to the Indian nation and the Tamil people. His prescient publisher's note to *Kannan Pattu* is justly famous.

> The Tamil people know of Bharati but few know his true greatness. Bharati is a genius. A great scholar. A *jeevan muktar*. The Tagore of Tamilnadu. A blessing to the Tamil country.
>
> Please do not mistake these words for undue exaltation. The high pedestal that I have put him on is his due. Those who do not realize this now will do so later.
>
> ...
>
> Let me add but one word: After his time, after many centuries, I can see in my mind's eye the women and men of the Tamil country rejoicing in his songs.

In another preface written at the same time, he requested readers not to 'underestimate the greatness of the book by its appearance. They deserve to be set in gems on leaves of gold.'

Within a week of his release from prison, Bharati wrote to Nellaiyappa Pillai in December 1918 urging him to reprint his books, and he promptly complied. This was the only time that Bharati's books would be reprinted in his lifetime. Bharati had been prolific during his exile, with over a score of manuscripts awaiting publication. While Nellaiyappa Pillai's means were moderate, Bharati had no means at all and a family to support.

Swallowing his pride, in May 1919 Bharati wrote two verse epistles to none other than the zamindar of Ettayapuram from whose employ he had walked out fifteen years earlier. The zamindar replied with silence. Bharati grew desperate and three months later wrote another letter, this time in prose. He stooped low, offering to rewrite 'in good, sweet, and clear Tamil' the royal genealogy of the zamin. The zamindar's stony silence to Bharati's overtures stopped the poet dead in his tracks. A little later, Bharati made one last-ditch effort, this time to seek the patronage of a Nattukkottai Chettiar merchant and banker but nothing came of his plans.

Finally, towards the end of his life, Bharati made a grandiose plan to publish all his works, the accumulated labour of his exile. In mid-1920 he issued two prospectuses of his plans – in English and in Tamil – and appealed for loans and donations. This was Bharati's scheme: to publish his books in forty volumes and print a first run of 10,000 copies each. He was sure his books would be 'sold as freely and quickly as kerosene or matchboxes'.

Most of the works which I have now selected for publication are prose-stories, sensational and, at the same time, classical; very easy, lucid, clear, luminous, and all but too popular in style and diction and, at the same time, chaste, pure, correct, epic, and time-defying. This fact and (2) the ever-growing increase of Tamil-reading men, women, and children in the Tamil world overseas; (3) the historic necessity of my works for the uplift of the Tamil land which, again, is a sheer necessity of the inevitable, imminent, and heaven-ordained Revival of the East; (4) the novel and American-like improvement which I propose to make in the printing, binding, and get-up of my editions—which, added [to] by beautiful and suitable pictures illustrating the interesting events occurring in the stories, will make them a tremendous attraction to our public and such a wondrous surprise; (5) the comparatively low price of my books: for I am going to sell my prose-works uniformly at 8 annas a copy and my poems at, so far possible, 4 annas a copy; and (6) my high reputation and unrivalled popularity in the Tamil-reading world due to my past publications—all these are bound most evidently to make my sales a prodigious success.

Bharati estimated that the plans would require Rs 20,000 for production costs and Rs 10,000 for advertising expenses. Priced at half a rupee a copy, the turnover would be Rs 200,000. Predicting such returns,

Bharati offered to pay twenty-four per cent annual interest on the loans contracted. Need one say that Bharati's plan was a non-starter.

Bharati was caught in between the end of the age of patronage and the beginning of a public market for literature. Tragically, both patrons and public alike spurned him.

During his lifetime, only about 150 of Bharati's 250 poems were printed. Of these less than half were collected and published in book form. Most importantly, a good half of his 'three great poems'– *Kannan Pattu, Panchali Sabatham* and *Kuyil* – remained unpublished at the time of his death. While *Kannan Pattu* saw a reissue, only the first half of *Panchali Sabatham* was published, and *Kuyil*, not at all. His prose writings, either scattered in various journals or still in manuscript form, presented an even more complicated picture. These include his celebrated translation of the Bhagavad Gita into Tamil.

In late 1920 Bharati returned to *Swadesamitran* as subeditor. Contemporary memoirs do not paint a happy picture of the poet. Tilak was dead, and Bharati was soon converted to the creed of Gandhian non-violence. Bharati had barely settled in Chennai when, on his usual visit to the Parthasarathy Temple in Triplicane, the temple elephant pushed him, traumatizing his already weak body. Though he continued to write columns, stories and poems, mostly in *Swadesamitran,* he was but a pale shadow of his former self.

In September 1921, he fell ill. A little past midnight, in the early hours of 12 September, Bharati died, at the age of thirty-nine. Fewer than a dozen attended his funeral. Only two obituaries have been traced so far. Death, however, brought Bharati an afterlife that perhaps the poet himself would never have dreamed of.

2

The Afterlife of a Master Spirit

If the publishing history of Bharati's writings in his own lifetime was a tragedy, then 'the story of the publication of the poet's works is a pretty long one, bordering on romance', his half-brother and posthumous publisher would observe.

In the decades leading up to the independence of India, Bharati's works, ignored when he was alive, grew increasingly popular. As the Indian freedom struggle strengthened in the couple of decades just after Bharati's death, his songs 'served as a battle-cry and rallying force in processions, in picketing and on the pulpit to lend colour to the political leaders' speeches'. This was especially so during the movement to boycott the Simon Commission and during the Civil Disobedience Movement in the late 1920s and early 1930s. Political meetings often began and ended with the singing of his songs. As many contemporary observers have recorded, the easiest way to mobilize a crowd was to sing a song or two of Bharati; it also usually ended in a decent collection of coins as the hat went around. The songs made the blood boil and tightened the sinews of the idealist youth who listened to them.

In 1928 the government of Burma, then still part of British India, banned Bharati's books for sedition, and the Madras government, according to imperial law, was bound to do the same in the presidency. But instead of smothering Bharati's poems, the ban increased their popularity. It became a testament to how important his songs were to Tamil political discourse. An adjournment motion was quickly moved in the Madras legislature. Discussions were dominated by the unconditional support Bharati was garnering, and the Madras government was forced to lift the ban.

Bharati's writings not only fuelled Indian nationalist sentiment but also played a seminal role in fashioning a Tamil identity. His songs on the glory of the Tamil language, the Tamil people and the land of the Tamils underpinned the emergence of a nascent identity politics.

The Afterlife of a Master Spirit

In the early 1930s, self-consciously modern writing emerged in Tamil. Bharati was frequently invoked and celebrated as the progenitor of Tamil modernity, becoming a key figure in its formation. This indicates the growing influence of Bharati outside of narrow political mobilization and on civil society at large. As his books were published through the 1920s and 1930s by Bharati Prachuralayam (whose genesis will be discussed later), modern Tamil writers found new sustenance for their writings and their sensibility. During this time, many periodicals frequently reprinted newly rediscovered writings of Bharati. Some journals carried his poems with illustrations. Journals such as *Manikodi* and *Suthanthira Sangu* drew their names from Bharati's poems, while journals like *Jayabharati* and *Balabharati* even suffixed 'Bharati' to their titles. There was even a monthly called *Bharati*. Invariably, journal banners carried lines from his poems as their epigraphs. *Dinamani*, a popular Tamil daily till this day, was launched on Bharati's birthday in 1933. Kanaga Subburathinam, who began as a nationalist poet and later dominated the Tamil poetry scene, called himself Bharatidasan (Bharati's disciple). Another poet adopted the nom de plume Balabharati. As a tribute to Bharati, suffixing the name 'Bharati' to fashion a nom de plume was not uncommon among writers, especially poets, during the 1930s and later.

Who Owns That Song?

As Bharati became a central figure in the making of modern Tamil culture, various stakeholders across the ideological spectrum sought to appropriate him. Some, like the prolific nationalist writer Kalki, downplayed Bharati's radicalism by claiming him to be merely a patriotic poet. Bharatidasan, associated with the Dravidian Movement, underplayed Bharati's anti-British orientation and focused instead on his social reform and anti-caste agenda. Conservatives such as C. Rajagopalachari (Rajaji) wanted to reduce him to a Vedantic poet due to the presence of strong Hindu elements in his poetry. Communists and socialists focused on his anti-colonial and anti-imperialist perspective and the emphasis he placed on speaking up against economic exploitation and poverty. For literary modernists he was the herald of modernity – free verse in Tamil was directly inspired by Bharati's prose poems. In short, Bharati became all things to all people. Perhaps the only consensus the debates on Bharati offered was that he was indeed a 'mahakavi' (great poet). His poetry having become absolutely seminal to the Tamil people, attention turned to Bharati's life. Biographies, then still a somewhat new genre, of Bharati began to proliferate during the 1930s and after. Quotations, citations and allusions to Bharati became ubiquitous in Tamil writing by the 1930s. The commercial implications of this new-found interest in Bharati would be profound and complex.

The Widow

When Bharati died, he left behind nothing for his family. His wife, Chellamma (c. 1890–1955), was barely thirty. She had two daughters, sixteen-year-old Thangammal (1905–71) and twelve-year-old Shakuntala (1909–76), to support.

Chellamma hailed from Kadayam, which, unlike the dry Ettayapuram 120 km to its east, was a lush village in the foothills of the Western Ghats. When they got married Bharati was fifteen, and Chellamma was barely seven. She probably never went to school. She would begin a note on her husband shortly after his death with the moving words 'I'm but an unlettered woman'.

In those days, child marriages were common, if not the norm, especially among Brahmins – post-puberty marriages brought social ostracism, if they did not actually land the offending bride's father in hellfire. Marriages were elaborate affairs, lasting for five days or more. For the bride and groom, it was supposed to be great fun. The bride repaired to her natal home immediately after the wedding ceremony; once the marriage was consummated

Bharati with wife Chellamma, an uncommon intimate pose for their time.

post her puberty, the husband would bring her to his house. Household life would commence in the husband's joint family under the watchful eyes of the mother-in-law. In Bharati and Chellamma's case, their separation after marriage was further extended by Chinnaswamy Iyer's death a year after the wedding. Orphaned, Bharati was forced to discontinue his studies in Tirunelveli and proceed to Varanasi.

When news of Bharati's radicalization in Varanasi and its outward manifestation in his hairstyle and clothes reached Bharati's young wife, she was terrified. Egged on by her alarmed family, Chellamma wrote a tearful letter to her husband. Bharati swiftly reassured her: addressing her as '*kadhali*' or beloved, he asked her not to be carried away by scaremongering relatives, as quoted from memory by Chellamma in her biography of her husband written in 1944. The letter ended with a characteristic Bharati flourish: 'At such moments of anxiety, if you study Tamil literary works, I shall be very happy.'

The marriage was consummated on Bharati's return from Varanasi. What the young girl made of her genius husband, and of his erratic habits and radical politics, is difficult to judge. She was often embarrassed by his public demonstration of love. Bharati addressed some of his love poems to Chellamma by name, and he had to later revise it to Kannamma. Sometimes he took her out for walks, and a surviving photograph shows the poet with his hand over her shoulders, a very uncommon pose for the times. Bharati looked for an idealistic companionate marriage, and perhaps Chellamma never came to terms with this.

Chellamma's life with Bharati was punctuated by two pregnancies and deliveries in her natal home. In early 1905 their first daughter Thangammal was born, and mother and child joined Bharati in Chennai where he was a budding cultural figure of the Swadeshi Movement. The four years or so following Thangammal's birth were the most hectic in the poet's life. Bharati's journalistic hands were full, and he was also involved in active politics: giving political talks and reciting poems at public meetings, organizing political associations and meetings, travelling to Calcutta, Varanasi, Surat, Rajahmundry and various towns in Tamilnadu on political work. Despite the possible stress caused by such political activity, this was probably the only time in her wedded life when Chellamma may not have had financial worries.

When Bharati sought political refuge in Pondicherry following a brutal crackdown on the Swadeshi Movement, Chellamma was pregnant for the second time. It was in this situation that Bharati dropped the idea of emigrating to Europe; what might have happened to the budding young poet and the future of Tamil cultural modernity had he become a revolutionary émigré is a big 'if' question.

The Afterlife of a Master Spirit

When the news of the birth of his second daughter came, Bharati was engrossed in reading Kalidasa, and promptly named her Shakuntala.

Chellamma soon joined her husband in exile with her two daughters. Racked by anxieties and fears, the Pondicherry years were a roller-coaster ride for her. When the papers were shut down, the family lost its steady source of income. Both the constant surveillance of the secret police and the harassment by its informers were aggravated by the endemic violence of local municipal politics. Chellamma found support from the families of fellow exiles.

For all his eccentricities, Bharati was a benevolent husband and encouraged his wife to read and write. Some of his own writings published in *Swadesamitran* ran with the byline 'Chellamma Bharati, wife of Subramania Bharati'. Straitened financial circumstances and the trying political climate adversely affected Bharati, and this must have reflected in his relationship with his wife. When the already bohemian and non-conformist Bharati took to spiritual and tantric exercises as well, he began to keep the company of many outcaste gurus with matted hair, dirty bodies and strange habits, and he also became addicted to opium. The turmoil this must have caused Chellamma can scarcely be imagined.

When Bharati decided to step out of Pondicherry in

November 1918, Chellamma must have been relieved. After twenty-five days of imprisonment in Cuddalore jail, Bharati rejoined his wife in her ancestral home.

The two years (or less) that he spent there must have been trying for him. He sought every opportunity to secure financial support but it came to nothing. After his failure to win the Ettayapuram zamindar's patronage, he reached out to the rich Nattukkottai Chettiar, Vai.Su. Shanmugam Chettiar, who was prepared to back his admiration for Bharati with money. It was now Chellamma's turn not to cooperate. Unconvinced by her fickle-minded husband, she refused to leave the relative security of her father's home for an untested patron. Bharati had to turn down the Chettiar's support when his wife refused to join him.

The tension in the family can be discerned by how their daughter Thangammal's marriage was conducted. Bharati had idealistic, if impractical, notions of how to arrange and conduct a marriage, such as the girl having a choice in who she got married to. But Chellamma's family did not let him have any say in the matter and Bharati just about marked his presence at his own daughter's wedding.

By the end of 1920, Bharati had managed to join *Swadesamitran* as an assistant editor. It was a climbdown, no doubt, but if Chellamma had felt relieved that things were settling down, it was not to be. In September 1921 Bharati died.

The Afterlife of a Master Spirit

Traditionally, Brahmin families forced widows to tonsure their heads, wear a drab *narmadi* sari without a blouse and observe strict dietary restrictions. The widow's life was one of deep humiliation and she was seen as an ill-starred and inauspicious figure. The many pictures of Chellamma after Bharati's death are a testament to her tragedy. She outlived Bharati by more than three decades and died in 1955.

~

All Bharati had left behind were some published books and many notebooks of manuscripts and files of paper clippings. The only possible source of income for the family were these writings. Therefore, within months of Bharati's death, Chellamma and her elder brother K.R. Appadurai Iyer launched a publishing concern called Bharati Ashramam.

A few years younger than Bharati, Appadurai Iyer had stood by his sister through the most difficult times. A patriotic man, Appadurai Iyer left a steady job in the postal department to join the freedom struggle. A great admirer of his brother-in-law's writings, he assisted him in the running of his journals. Arrested in December 1911, possibly for links to the murder of Collector Ashe, he was released a month later. It is clear from police reports that he was under constant surveillance. When Bharati stepped out of Pondicherry and was arrested in Cuddalore, Appadurai Iyer accompanied Bharati and Chellamma and was involved in getting him released, including negotiating with the deputy inspector general of police, Patrick Hannyngton.

It was this trusted brother who lent a helping hand to Chellamma in running the publishing firm. And, as fate would have it, this very enterprise would drive a wedge between the siblings.

Two weeks after Bharati's death, Chellamma issued a public appeal for funds to support her publishing programme. Not much was raised but a contribution from the Tilak Swaraj Fund, which was set up at the instance of Gandhi during the Non-Cooperation Movement to help in the freedom struggle, and donations from the Rangoon public and others helped her to bring out these volumes. Within five months of Bharati's death, Bharati Ashramam published two volumes of his poems, titled *Swadesa Geethangal*, parts one and two. Priced at a rupee each, the two volumes together contained 170 songs and ran into 300 pages, exclusive of preliminary pages with informative introductions and forewords. The books had a print run of 3000 each.

To the first volume, Chellamma wrote an extraordinarily moving preface. 'I'm but an unlettered woman,' she began,

The Afterlife of a Master Spirit

'I do not venture to introduce this book. Nor do I have the ability to. There are lakhs of men and women like me in this Tamil country. I want to say a word to them,' and continued, 'My husband . . . Subramania Bharati was born in this country, and performed all his tasks in a great hurry, and when his time approached, he died as if dying too was a hurried task.' After briefly describing his writing career, she ended her preface with the remark: 'I've sworn that, until my end comes, I shall take the responsibility of publishing Bharati's works in full and later relinquish it in favour of Tamilnadu.'

Fate willed otherwise. Within a few years of writing these words, Chellamma would lose all control over her husband's writings, while others profited from his works. The copyright fell into the public domain in her own lifetime.

Chellamma's Bharati Ashramam venture was a disaster. Her brother, who had stood behind her and Bharati during the most trying of times, fell out with her, an indication perhaps of the magnitude of the financial loss and the difficulties of running a publishing firm. Following his departure, the accounts were left in a mess and Chellamma had no clue about who owed what. The books remained unsold in heavy bundles and gathered dust in her Triplicane home, a visual testimony to the failure of the publishing venture.

The bundles were soon moved to the Hindi Prachar Sabha office by Pandit Harihara Sarma, a family friend. Sarma promised Chellamma a monthly subsistence from the proceeds of the sales. Meanwhile, attempts were made to sell the entire copyright but the responses were not encouraging, with the best offer being Rs 3000 and that too in instalments.

By then the marriage of the younger daughter had to be performed. After some failed prospective alliances and considerable difficulties, Shakuntala's marriage with K. Natarajan – who would later become a partner in publishing Bharati – became possible in 1924 only by pledging the copyright for a loan. In this task, Chellamma was assisted by C. Visvanathan, Bharati's half-brother, and Sarma. Her natal family having forsaken Chellamma, she turned to her husband's family.

The loan taken to perform the marriage, as Visvanathan observed, 'could not be discharged nor a provision made for the poet's family'. It was at this juncture, in 1924, that Visvanathan began publishing Bharati himself under Bharati Prachuralayam. Sarma and Natarajan joined him as partners in this publishing firm devoted exclusively to publishing Bharati. Evidently, Chellamma Bharati was paid royalties till the time the copyright was bought from her.

The forfeiture of the stocks of books by the government

following the proscription of Bharati's poems (1928), a major commercial calamity, soon turned to be a blessing in disguise. The heated debate in the Madras Legislative Assembly to oppose the proscription and the public sensation that this caused fanned the fire of Bharati's popularity. When the government revoked the ban, the forfeited copies were returned and sold, rather ingeniously, with the stamp 'This Copy was Seized by Govt. on 20th Sep. 1928. Forfeiture Order Cancelled and Book Returned 22-1-1929'. (It is said that such stamping was done even on copies printed later.) In any case, this controversy increased sales.

Perhaps this emboldened Bharati Prachuralayam to purchase the entire copyright in 1931 for a sum of Rs 4000 to be paid in instalments to Chellamma. Until then it had been publishing books on a royalty basis. Visvanathan justified this deal later in the following terms: 'It is a low sum indeed but considering the value of Bharati's works in those days, the offers that were made then and our own financial position, it was decent enough.'

After this arrangement, a steady stream of publications issued from Bharati Prachuralayam. As editions sold out, new impressions were produced. Between 1924 and 1935 about twenty-five of Bharati's books were published. Not only were earlier books reissued but new titles based on the manuscripts and paper clippings left behind by the poet were also published. Visvanathan added to the list by scouring various journals and reviews and ferreted out Bharati's writings, a task that involved considerable effort.

While the sincerity of Visvanathan and his publishing house to unearth Bharati's works and make them available need not be doubted, that there was a growing market for Bharati was undeniable. Considering the nature of Bharati's writings – their anti-colonial tenor and nationalist content – the risk of drawing police attention by publishing them cannot be discounted. But Visvanathan's statement, 'Our office was searched on several occasions, our files seized, our books confiscated. Personally, I was shadowed and my letters were intercepted and I was forbidden from entering Government service,' was somewhat exaggerated.

Since Bharati's books could not be prescribed as school textbooks, then a major source of livelihood for publishers, different strategies had to be pursued to promote sales. Liberal discounts to booksellers and concessions to educational institutions were offered. As much as fifty per cent commission was given to organizations celebrating Bharati Day, which in itself was one more indication of the celebrity status that the poet was now acquiring.

Over the years Bharati Prachuralayam came solely into the hands of Visvanathan when his two partners left him one after the other, Natarajan in 1938 and Sarma in 1941. According to Visvanathan, the former left as 'it was not a paying business' and the latter 'for other reasons', presumably differences over conducting business.

Broadcast Rights Change Hands

The early 1930s saw what has been described as a 'music boom' by Stephen P. Hughes, historian of Tamil cinema. From the late 1920s, sound reprographic devices became available and grew in popularity. During this time, Bharati's songs were part of not only patriotic theatre but also of commercial plays which had to reckon with the rising nationalist consciousness and mobilization. Consequently, new considerations entered the scene. Probably to capitalize on this and perhaps to raise more money to augment resources, Bharati Prachuralayam sold the broadcast rights. An agreement was signed in 1934 with Jeshinglal K. Mehta. Visvanathan later recalled that this assignment was initiated by Sarma without his knowledge.

Who was this Mehta? He was born in Gujarat in August 1901. A jeweller, he was a partner in Messrs Surajmal Lallubhai & Co. with 'extensive and lucrative business in diamond and jewelleries in India and outside'. It had branches in Bombay, Trichy and Rangoon, and dealt in gold, diamond and silver ornaments. In Chennai the firm functioned out of 313, Esplanade from 1922.

The agreement with Mehta was towards 'partial assignment of the rights to make records in gramophone and in talkies and any other sound producing broadcast device' for a lump sum of Rs 450 and a royalty of one anna per record sold. No details are available about any royalties that he may have remitted to Bharati Prachuralayam. Apparently, Mehta made no use of the rights that he acquired, and nothing was heard of them until a decade later.

By 1946 the worth of Bharati's songs had been better recognized and its commercial value had increased manyfold. It was at this juncture, as Indian independence was imminent, that the movie mogul AV. Meiyappa Chettiar entered the scene, hoping to cash in on Bharati's popularity, by using his songs in a forthcoming film.

The Movie Mogul

The Nattukkottai Chettiars, a small but influential community of traders, moneylenders and bankers, were once concentrated in Chettinadu, as the region is informally known, in the dry interior of central Tamilnadu. While the community traces its history to the classical Tamil epic *Silappadhikaram*, there is evidence of their trading interest in southeast Asia in the early modern period. By the latter half of the nineteenth century, as European powers opened up the region in pursuit of their colonial interests, the Chettiars made deep inroads into Sri Lanka, Burma, Malaya, Cambodia and Indonesia. Trading and moneylending in faraway lands came with enormous risks, and the Chettiars earned admiration, tempered by envy, for their sharp skills and shrewd manoeuvring, which were accompanied by a strong sense of community. Legends, folk tales, proverbs and sayings attest to this popular perception. (Here is one: A Chettiar moneylender to an unlettered client wanting to settle his loan account: 'Ten tens make a hundred and ten. Let me waive ten. It's enough if you pay a hundred.') They were also known for their meticulous bookkeeping, which was meant to both reveal and conceal.

Chettiar was a caste surname taken by a range of castes involved in trading, including the Nattukkottai Chettiars, though they preferred to call themselves Nagarathars. Avinashilingam Chettiar, for instance, who will soon figure in our story, or for that matter India's first finance minister R.K. Shanmugam Chettiar, did not belong to this community.

Like many communities reliant on speculative wealth and usury, they were known for their philanthropy. They endowed temples, contributed liberally to temple rituals and built free inns for pilgrims. The community faced a severe crisis during the Great Depression in the early 1930s and the years leading up to World War II. The Japanese conquest of southeast Asia and the rebellious mood of decolonization were catastrophic for the community, and both capital and people fled to the homeland and found their way into a range of businesses, not excluding cinema and publishing.

AV. Meiyappan was born in 1907 in Karaikudi, the primary urban centre of Chettinadu. Meiyappan's grandfather had business interests in Burma but his father, Avichi Chettiar, preferred to set up shop in his home town. Rather than engaging in moneylending, he opened A.V. & Sons, a firm that sold and distributed a range of goods, which Meiyappan calls a veritable department store in his memoir.

Meiyappan joined his father and quickly learnt the trade. In 1928 A.V. & Sons took up the authorized distribution of gramophone records – especially of classical music performed by stars like S.G. Kittappa and K.B. Sundarambal – for the five southern districts of the Madras Presidency. In 1932, in partnership with two others, Meiyappan established Saraswathi Stores, which would go on to become a leading name in music distribution for over half a century. Saraswathi Stores entered into a contract with Odeon Records, a leading German company, to distribute gramophone records all over South India. Apart from classical music, Meiyappan also diversified into popular songs.

From gramophone to talkies was but a logical next step, and it was not long before the seductive celluloid siren caught the young man's fancy. After over a decade of silent films, the Tamil talkie made its debut in 1931 with *Kalidas*. As Meiyappan confessed in his memoir, he was overtaken by curiosity and developed an 'itch' for the new medium. In the next three years, the enterprising young man, under the banner of Saraswathi Sound Production, produced a film, shot entirely in New Theatres Studio, Calcutta. After the whole film was produced at a cost of Rs 80,000, he found that the hero's eyes were half closed through most of the film because of the glare of the arc lights. That *Alli Arjuna* failed surprised no one, not least its own producer.

Undeterred, Meiyappan launched his next project. *Ratnavali* (1936), with an outlay of 1.5 lakh rupees, was also shot in Calcutta but this time in Pioneer Studios. Meiyappan experimented with a new camera. Though it yielded technically superior images, the new camera shot at a different speed, a fact that went unnoticed by the sound recordist. The sound therefore did not sync, causing an unintended comic effect. *Nandakumar*, produced the next year in Pune, bombed as well.

Who Owns That Song?

Three back-to-back initial flops is scarcely the formula for what would become the cinema company that would continue to dominate the Tamil film industry, three-quarters of a century after its inception. Meiyappan did not give up easily. Concluding that having his own studio was the answer to his troubles, he embarked on building one. After toying with the idea of locating his studio in Bangalore, he finally opened Pragati Studios in Chennai, at the Admiralty House. The house was rumoured to be haunted, and Meiyappan could therefore rent it. Superstition notwithstanding, the studio delivered a series of hits.

In 1941 Meiyappan ventured into direction and filmed *Sabapathy*, the first full-length comedy in Tamil cinema. It proved to be a runaway success. More than seventy-five years after its first release, *Sabapathy* is still watchable, not something that can be said of many films of those times.

Meiyappan had an uncanny ability to spot talent. If he introduced T.R. Mahalingam in his first box-office hit, *Sri Valli* (1945) (which also introduced the award-winning actress Lakshmi's mother Rukmini), Marcus Bartley, the cinematographer, was also Meiyappan's find. He introduced Vyjayanthimala Bali to the film world with *Vazhkai* (1948); her Hindi debut, *Bahaar*, followed soon after, also under the AVM banner, his eponymous company. The Travancore sisters, Lalitha and Padmini, first appeared on screen in an AVM film. All these actors would go on to become stars of their time. Though Meiyappan may have wanted to forget that Waheeda Rehman failed an AVM screen test.

Meiyappan successfully handled the wartime evacuation of Chennai city for fear of Japanese aerial bombing, as well as the government-imposed restriction of film-reel length to 11,000 feet from the usual 20,000-odd feet to deal with scarcity of film stock. After the war, due to disagreements with his partners, Pragati Studio changed hands. Meiyappan's attempts to start a new studio in Chennai failed as the electricity company refused to supply power to new firms as a post-war austerity measure.

In a daring move, Meiyappan opened his new studio, AVM, in out-of-the-way Karaikudi in 1946. It was here that he decided to produce a social film, *Nam Iruvar*, based on a successful play. During the war years and immediately after, hoarding and black marketing were rampant, and Meiyappan decided that a film on that theme would find immediate resonance with the audience. Meiyappan, who until then – over a period of twelve years when he was involved in film business at the peak of nationalist activity – had displayed no inclination towards the freedom struggle, decided that using Bharati's songs would make sound marketing sense. As he recalled later,

> It's important, in the making of films, to keep the storyline in tune with the times. In my *Nam Iruvar*, made at the time of Indian independence, I included Mahakavi Bharati's songs, and they became a big hit. What's there to talk about independence now!

It was at this juncture that he asked around to acquire 'the rights of reproduction by gramophone, broadcasting, and other sound-producing devices of the songs, works, and compositions of the late C. Subramanya Bharathi'.

It took Meiyappan many wide-ranging enquiries to discover that the rights were held by Jeshinglal Mehta. With a well-padded wallet Meiyappan met Mehta, hoping to clinch the deal in the smug belief that the Gujarati businessman would want to get rid of what had become a dead investment.

But Mehta was no ordinary businessman. It was a war of wits between the Nattukkottai Chettiar and the Gujarati Bania. Since Mehta had bought the rights for only Rs 450, Meiyappan hoped to take it off his hands for 'three or four thousand rupees' and, as he admitted in his memoir, he 'employed every business trick' to peg the deal at that price. But Mehta would not budge: perhaps realizing that this was his one chance to make the best of a dead investment of over a dozen years, he struck a tough bargain. Meiyappan was the first to blink, and finally settled for the substantial sum of Rs 9500, though in the end he was not unhappy. The agreement was signed in September 1946, a quarter-century after Bharati's death.

Nam Iruvar (1947) proved to be a success beyond Meiyappan's wildest dreams. The rising dancing star Kumari Kamala – later sometime wife of the cartoonist R.K. Laxman – sashaying to Bharati's song '*Aaduvome pallu paduvome*', prophetically heralding the coming of freedom to India, rendered by D.K. Pattammal, was the single most important moment in the film that drew repeat audiences to the cinema hall.

In 1948, following Partition, AVM Studios acquired an evacuee property and moved to Chennai, where it continues to function to this day. Meiyappan's stars continued to rise in the following years and decades. C.N. Annadurai's *Or Iravu*, Sivaji Ganesan's astonishing debut *Parasakti*, and many other blockbuster films were made. Meiyappan also produced many Hindi films such as *Bhai-Bhai, Chori Chori, Hum Panchhi Ek Daal Ke* and *Bhabhi*. By the 1950s, AVM, along with S.S. Vasan's Gemini Studios, easily dominated South Indian cinema with a foot in the Hindi film world as well.

Meiyappan's acquisition of the broadcast and recording

rights of Bharati's works was the fountainhead of the controversy that led to the nationalization of Bharati. What had earned the movie mogul windfall profits would soon draw him into a controversy, and a crisis. He would have to rely on his keen business acumen and understanding of politics not only to save the day but also to convert a possible calamity into an opportunity.

3

Make it Public!

By the turn of the 1940s, Bharati's widespread influence on the emergent public sphere was palpable. His writings were widely used in public discourse. Even though Bharati Prachuralayam claimed that 'permission to include a few lines and a few stanzas or even whole poems in text books ha[d] been given on a nominal royalty basis or free according to the nature of the applicant' and that private bodies such as The Servants of India Society had been given free permission to bring out their own selections, it obviously was not enough to meet the growing need for Bharati's poems.

Consequently, a few disparate voices, with the demand to make Bharati's works public property, could be heard. In the First Conference of Tamil Writers held in Coimbatore in November 1944, a resolution was proposed by A.V.R. Krishnaswamy Reddiar, a prominent literary personality, for 'rescuing the poems of Bharati from the clutches of private individuals'. It is difficult to imagine how this entirely unprecedented demand to nationalize the works of a writer was conceived, articulated and voiced. This demand was reiterated in the next conference of Tamil writers in December 1946 in Chennai. And as the campaign to nationalize Bharati's works gained momentum, this cry became even stronger in the third conference held in Nagercoil in May 1948.

The demand for nationalization acquired considerable force in October 1947 during the inauguration of the Bharati Manimantapam – a decorative hall constructed with public subscriptions raised through a popular campaign – at Ettayapuram. The traditional 'groundbreaking ceremony' for this hall, on 3 June 1945, was itself a grand affair organized by Kalki, with Rajaji's blessings. This was the first time the poet was being feted at his birthplace.

A galaxy of political and literary figures landed in Ettayapuram in October 1947 to celebrate the poet and his work, and of course, to appropriate him. In subsequent years this little town would suffer from celebration fatigue, with its residents unable to attend the plethora of events held periodically.

Though writers and personalities from across the political and ideological spectrum were invited (there were, of course, a few controversial exceptions like Bharatidasan and Va.Ra.), it was a show dominated by Rajaji, who had recently taken over as the first Indian governor of West Bengal, and his clique. And as it often happens in such events, Bharati's family – his widow and daughters, and his half-brother – were neither properly invited nor honoured.

The event was not only a Bharati festival but also a deferred celebration of Indian independence. In the general euphoria and mood of festivity, P. Jeevanandam's speech stood out – and to some ears, it struck a jarring note.

Born in Bhoodapandi, now in the Kanyakumari district of Tamilnadu, and in what was then the Tamil-speaking region of the native state of Travancore, Jeeva (as he was fondly called) was one of the most distinguished Tamil orators of the twentieth century. He made the transition to the age of microphone brilliantly. It is said that he spoke so loudly into the megaphone that his eardrums burst and consequently he became hard of hearing. As a young man attracted to Indian nationalism and inspired by Gandhi, he established an ashram in the Mahatma's name near Karaikudi. In the late 1920s he joined Periyar's Self-Respect Movement, a stridently anti-caste and anti-religion social reform project. Periyar, after his year-long visit to the Soviet Union and Europe in 1931–32, took a socialist path, which greatly appealed to Jeeva. The young Jeeva, then only in his twenties, played a stellar role in the movement, writing poems, essays and propaganda. In 1934, when Periyar gave up his socialistic propaganda, Jeeva was part of a breakaway group critical of Periyar and joined the Congress Socialist Party. In the latter half of the 1930s Jeeva was the public face of the Communist Party of India (CPI), editing the party journal *Janasakthi*, organizing workers and mobilizing support. A selfless man, usually dressed in shorts (it is said that he took to wearing a four-yard *vetti* only after he became an MLA following an election he won when he was virtually underground), he was also a scholar with an enviable talent for reciting poems. Almost single-handedly, Jeeva reinterpreted and presented Bharati as a radical poet committed to progressive social change rather than a narrow nationalist writer on religious and philosophical themes. That Bharati was the only Indian poet to write welcoming the Russian Revolution strengthened his argument. His public speeches were packed with information interpreted from a socialistic perspective and was an alternative to the new form of public speaking – neoclassical (in its revival of an ancient style) and alliterative – being fashioned by the Dravidian Movement.

Make it Public!

A merciless critic of Rajaji and his politics, Jeeva was one of the last speakers to be called to the podium at the inauguration of the Bharati Manimantapam. But his talk elicited quite a response and fuelled the campaign for the nationalization of Bharati's works:

> The publication rights of Bharati's books are in [Bharati's half-brother] Mr Visvanathan's hands. The rights to use them in films, on radio, and on gramophone have been purchased by Meiyappa Chettiar.
>
> Bharati's writings are the common property of the Tamils, nay, of the whole world. Like Gandhi's writings* Bharati's writings too need to be made public property, and the Tamil people and the government should take necessary steps to free them from private hands.

Reciting an appropriate verse from Bharati that called for the Tamil language to be sounded on the streets if the Tamil people were to thrive, he called upon Visvanathan to give up his rights voluntarily. If he did so, Jeeva said, 'the people would remain eternally grateful to him'. If, on the other hand, he decided 'to stand by his rights with a desire to make money', Jeeva warned, 'blame would befall him'.

---

* Jeeva was mistaken about Gandhi's writing being nationalized; that wasn't the case.

Who Owns That Song?

While this is the official version of his speech published on the occasion by the CPI's Janasakthi Press, Jeeva is said to have declared that if Visvanathan was particular about money, the required amount could be collected in quarter annas and half annas from the Tamil people and the coppers thrown on his face. Visvanathan was, understandably, offended by this suggestion. Jeeva made a similar demand to Meiyappan.

Even after such fervent pleas if Visvanathan and Meiyappan refused to heed the public, then Jeeva argued and vehemently demanded that the government take over the copyright. Should the state turn a deaf ear, he warned that 'the Tamil people would launch a systematic and belligerent agitation' to achieve their goal.

Jeeva's was the most forceful demand until then for the state takeover of Bharati's copyright. Undoubtedly, the mood immediately after independence was one of great expectation from the government – the citizens believed in the unbridled power of the government to intervene in every walk of life for the greater common good. It is worth remembering that, as a communist, Jeeva was committed to an ideology that negated private property and, at that time, his party was in direct conflict with the Congress government.

M.P. Sivagnanam, autodidact, eloquent orator, writer and a faction leader within the Congress, and Narana

Duraikannan, a middling if widely respected writer and journalist, are also said to have voiced the nationalization demand at this event, but it was Jeeva who stole the show.

On the day of the inauguration of the Bharati Manimantapam, Parali S. Nellaiyappa Pillai's talk was broadcast on All India Radio (AIR) to mark the event. 'It's been over a quarter of a century since Bharati left us. But despite the passage of so much time the songs of this liberation poet remain shackled by various chains,' he said, and called for 'declaring all of Bharati's poems and writings as public property and publishing them in lakhs of copies for distribution across the country'.

It was in this atmosphere that an apparently simple legal notice triggered off a series of events that ultimately led to the nationalization of Bharati's works.

Enter T.K. Shanmugam

T.K. Shanmugam (1912–73), born in Trivandrum, hailed from Nagercoil, some twenty miles from the southernmost tip of India, Kanyakumari. Though a Tamil-speaking region, for historical reasons it was then part of Travancore state, till it became a part of Madras state in 1956.

Shanmugam hailed from an acting family and was a student of Sankaradas Swamigal (1867–1922). Swamigal – an honorific suffix referring to one who has renounced worldly life – is considered the father of Tamil theatre.

The author of about fifty plays, he drew on pre-existing popular theatrical traditions full of songs and adapted his plays for the proscenium. Mythological and pseudo-historical themes formed the staple of his repertoire. In his days, women, with the exception of devadasis – a community of dancing girls dedicated to the temple – were wary of appearing on stage. To tide over the difficulty of finding women for the stage, Swamigal employed only boys, and they would play both male and female roles – a pioneering move. Thus was born Boys' Companies, an institution that dominated Tamil theatre in the early part of the twentieth century. It trained generations of actors – M.G. Ramachandran (MGR) and Sivaji Ganesan being only two of the most illustrious – who dominated not only theatre but also Tamil cinema.

Swamigal was an all-rounder, well versed in all aspects of theatre production. A legendary figure, the respect he won bordered on veneration. Shanmugam joined Swamigal's troupe at the age of six. Though he was the third of four brothers – Sankaran, Muthuswamy and Bhagavathi – who were also part of the troupe, the handsome Shanmugam was easily the most distinguished. Training under Swamigal was tough. Swamigal was a benevolent despot; a strict disciplinarian, he did not hesitate to thrash the boys if they did not measure up to his standards, though the diligent Shanmugam was spared the rod. The troupe travelled from town to town, all over the Tamil-speaking regions, and it was a tough if exhilarating life with performances starting late in the day and continuing into the small hours. There were no wigs, and boys grew their hair long. Talented boys were in demand, and rival troupes often poached on young talent with various enticements, sometimes resorting to kidnapping as well. When the boys approached puberty and their voice broke (called *magara-kattu*), their careers often ended disastrously.

Swamigal died in 1922, and a few years later, in 1925, Shanmugam and his brothers started their own theatre company, Madurai Sri Bala Shanmugananda Sabha, though popularly they were known as T.K.S. Bros.

During a visit to Bombay, Shanmugam saw Parsi plays for the first time and was impressed by the extravagant backdrops and quick changeover of scenes. He adopted these techniques and expanded the themes of his plays. From the predominantly mythological and pseudo-historical subjects replete with songs, which were the defining feature of Swamigal's plays, the repertoire now expanded with a focus on topics of social reform. M. Kandaswamy Mudaliar, MGR's earliest mentor, scripted many such plays. The range of his plays on social reform themes earned his company the sobriquet 'Seerthirutha Nataka Company' (Social Reform Drama Company).

Who Owns That Song?

In the wake of Bhagat Singh's martyrdom in 1931, Shanmugam was attracted to nationalist politics. He produced *Desabhakti*, an adapted version of the proscribed play *Banapurathu Veeran* by V. Swaminatha Sarma, written in the wake of the Jallianwala Bagh massacre. Staged within days of Bhagat Singh's execution, the Tirunelveli district administration banned it. In the 1937 provincial elections, Shanmugam campaigned for the Congress, which recorded a resounding victory.

Following the first Tamil talkie in 1931, cinema soon became the most popular art form, drawing talent and speculators, not to speak of spectators. But the early films were little more than mythological plays filmed on celluloid with a virtually immobile camera. In 1935 Shanmugam's *Menaka*, based on a popular novel by Vaduvur Duraiswamy Iyengar, was made into a film, and was the first social Tamil talkie. Shanmugam played the lead role, and with no woman to portray his love interest, his brother Muthuswamy enacted the role, bringing in another practice from theatre; men specializing in playing women's roles were called *stri-part*. Shot within thirty days in Bombay, *Menaka* turned out to be a big hit. However, despite his occasional forays into cinema, Shanmugam was committed to theatre and continued to be a theatre artist until his death in 1973.

Shanmugam's lasting fame rested on his title role of

Avvaiyar. Avvai ('ar' being an honorific suffix) is arguably Tamil's most popular woman poet. Such was her popularity that there are at least three Avvais in Tamil literary history, and numerous oral traditions accreted over time collapsing all the Avvais into one – as an old woman who wrote easily memorizable didactic verse. In 1942 Shanmugam blended these traditions into a single narrative and dramatized it into a play which was a resounding success. He removed two of his front teeth, curved his lower lip inward and played the role of the wise old woman brilliantly. Soon he came to be referred to as Avvai Shanmugam.

Shanmugam's commitment to social reform themes also won him Periyar's support. Not one for matters of art, Periyar nevertheless recognized the contribution of Shanmugam's plays towards sensitizing the people to the pressing social reform questions of the day. Not far behind was C.N. Annadurai, the rising star of Periyar's movement, who wrote a glowing review of Shanmugam's *Gumastavin Penn*.

Apart from his association with the Congress and the Self-Respect Movement, Shanmugam also had connections to the emerging Communist Party. Jeeva also hailed from Kanyakumari, and his agitprop, especially songs, caught Shanmugam's attention. The two soon became thick friends. Through Jeeva, Shanmugam also got to know such stalwarts of the Communist Party as A.K. Gopalan and K. Baladandayutham. When the party wanted to convert its weekly *Janasakthi* into a daily, Shanmugam extended generous financial assistance.

In the mid-1940s, like many intellectuals of his time, Shanmugam came under the spell of M.P. Sivagnanam. A thin man with a trademark bushy moustache, Sivagnanam came from a poor family of toddy tappers and sellers. Unschooled, he learnt Tamil even as he worked as a compositor in a printing press. A Congressman, he nevertheless championed the cause of a distinct Tamil identity within a larger Indian national identity, and made a political demand for state autonomy. Towards his distinct brand of politics, positioned against the secessionist programme of Periyar's Dravidar Kazhagam and Anna's Dravida Munnetra Kazhagam, he appropriated the Tamil classics, especially the epic *Silappadhikaram*, for this purpose. He also fashioned as icons the freedom fighters Veerapandiya Kattabomman and V.O. Chidambaram Pillai (Shanmugam staged as well as acted in a bio-play based on the latter) who were Indian and Tamil. His oratorical eloquence was an additional draw. In the years immediately following Indian independence he was in the forefront of the struggle for the linguistic reorganization of states, and for the retention of all Tamil-speaking areas within the Madras state. Sivagnanam was another key figure in the campaign for nationalizing Bharati.

Shanmugam was not without competitors in the world of theatre – but his troupe enjoyed a rare social respectability and cross-party support at a time when theatre was typically associated with vice, immorality and depravity.

Called to Court

It was to this respected theatre personality that Meiyappan sent a legal notice threatening to sue for copyright infringement if Shanmugam dared to use Bharati's songs in his film.

Shanmugam had been using Bharati's songs in his theatre productions from as early as the late 1920s. Following the success of his play *Bilhanan* (1948), based on the legendary eleventh-century Kashmiri poet of the same name, Shanmugam decided to turn it into a film. Bilhana's story – with its strong romantic element of a poor poet charming a beautiful princess with his mellifluous poetry – was quite popular, and had by then been adapted by many writers. A song from Bharati's *Kannàn Pattu*, '*Thoondil puzhuvinai pol*' (Like the worm in a bait – a song on the pining of a lover), which Shanmugam had used in the play, was to be included in the cinematic version as well.

On 29 January 1948, well before the release of the movie, Meiyappan issued a legal notice to Shanmugam stating that all recording rights of Bharati's songs vested solely with him and that no song may be used without his express permission. And if any song had been included in the film, he demanded its immediate deletion. If Shanmugam failed to do so, he threatened legal action and to claim for damages to the tune of Rs 50,000, an astronomical sum back then.

A shocked Shanmugam received the notice a few days after Gandhi's assassination. Before pursuing the legal route, Shanmugam chose to confront the issue politically. First, he composed a pamphlet wrought with emotion. The single-sheet leaflet titled *Bharati-kku Viduthalai Vendum!* (Needed: Liberation for Bharati!) asked pointedly and forcefully, 'Is it not shameful that in an independent India, some private individuals should claim title to the sweet poems of our Mahakavi?'

> Dear friends, you rejoiced by building a *manimantapam* for Mahakavi Bharati and commemorating Bharati Day. You desire that the immortal poet's songs should spread all over the world ... But have you realised that a hurdle has come up in our own country? Earlier the government imposed a ban. Now some individuals are imposing a ban.
>
> ... Leaders such as Rajaji had unanimously declared at the Ettayapuram function that people should proudly sing Bharati's songs.

But how are we to sing his songs? And where do we sing the songs? Are not individuals claiming them: 'It's my property! I own it!'... Is it right on your part to permit the immortal poet of Tamilnadu to be locked up in an iron safe and made a matter of business?

Even though legally this case has to be judged in a court of law, we have every right to ask the people living in a free country: Who owns Bharati?

Why should the Madras government not issue a proclamation that 'Bharati's poems and writings are the property of Tamilnadu. No individual has any right over it.'

The nation has become free. But is there no freedom for Mahakavi Bharati, who sang for the nation's liberation, even twenty-five years after his death?

Shanmugam articulated this unprecedented demand for state takeover of the copyright of Bharati's works using highly emotional language, which appealed to the freedom of the nation as well as the unity of the Tamil people. Bharati had come to represent both.

In this leaflet the focus was primarily on recording and broadcast rights, and the mention of publishing rights held by Visvanathan was made only in passing.

League for the Liberation of Bharati

To go back a little in time, in October 1947, a forum called Bharati Viduthalai Kazhagam (League for the Liberation of Bharati) had been formed following the demands raised at the inauguration of the Bharati Manimantapam. Though this league is credited with achieving the nationalization of Bharati's works, its genesis and functioning is unclear due to lack of documentation.

Ediroli Viswanathan, who wrote a short book on the story of Bharati's copyright and had access to the relevant file from Shanmugam, states that this was Narana Duraikannan's initiative and that he enrolled members and drafted pamphlets for the purpose.

The first meeting of the league was held on 11 March 1948. Prominent literary figures were present at the meeting. Va.Ra. was elected president; Narana Duraikannan and A. Srinivasa Raghavan, professor of English and a poet of some worth, were elected vice presidents. S.D.S. Yogi, a poet; Tiruloka Sitaram, Bharati enthusiast and passionate reciter of Bharati's poems; and Vallikannan, then an emerging writer and journalist and later a respected literary historian, were made secretaries.

The election, or rather nomination, of the office bearers was plagued by difficulties. Va.Ra. was turning sixty that year and, not unsurprisingly, for someone who had been a full-time Tamil writer and journalist, was in financial doldrums. A committee had been formed around this time to commemorate his birthday and the occasion was intended as a pretext to raise a purse. Meiyappan was a prospective patron, who, not to forget, was also the imminent target for the campaign to free Bharati from copyright. Hence Kalki is said to have struck down the decision to make Va.Ra. the president of the league. Eventually, the self-effacing Narana Duraikannan donned the mantle. This league is said to have toured all over Tamilnadu, mobilizing support to bring Bharati's works into the public domain.

The sequence is at variance with newly unearthed facts. It is now clear that the league's first meeting was held some six weeks after Meiyappan sent the legal notice to T.K.S. Bros. The league, despite its probable genesis before the legal fight over Bharati's copyright ensued, began its actual functioning after the legal furore.

Narana Duraikannan and Ediroli Viswanathan mention in their accounts of the battle for copyright that after Shanmugam's letters and Bharati Viduthalai Kazhagam's memorandum had reached the Madras premier Omandur Ramaswamy Reddiar's table, he had instructed T.S. Chockalingam, a respected journalist, to take some steps. There is, however, no reference to this in the government files. It was following this that Shanmugam, Narana Duraikannan and Raghavan left for Tirunelveli to meet Chellamma Bharati.

~

Given his standing in the public sphere, Shanmugam did not take Meiyappan's legal challenge lying down. He did not stop with sending letters to the government and printing leaflets. In mid-April 1948 he first went to Chennai and later to other parts of Tamilnadu, launching a public campaign for the government takeover of the copyright of Bharati's works.

Shanmugam met Narana Duraikannan in Chennai. Later he conferred with Va.Ra., Nellaiyappa Pillai and T.P. Meenakshisundaram. Va.Ra. had been a close confidant of Bharati from his Pondicherry days, and had penned the influential biography and character sketch of Bharati at the height of the 'mahakavi' controversy. Narana Duraikannan, despite not being a great writer, was widely respected for his humane qualities. A staunch believer in the power of writing to mould good human beings, he avoided confrontation and had the ability to handle people with strong viewpoints. As editor of *Prasanda Vikatan*, he had encouraged scores of writers, and was looked upon as an éminence grise. Nellaiyappa Pillai, a great admirer of Bharati and referred to by the poet himself as '*thambi*' (younger brother), had been his publisher in his own lifetime. T.P. Meenakshisundaram, renowned literary man and linguist, had a formidable reputation as a scholar. Shanmugam evolved a consensus among such widely respected cultural figures and sought their blessings and good wishes for the campaign to nationalize Bharati's writings.

Following this confabulation, Shanmugam's discussions with Narana Duraikannan and Vallikannan continued late into the night on the sands of Marina Beach. The next night, accompanied by the above two friends, he set out towards Tirunelveli on what came to be known as the Bharati Liberation Yatra. The group disembarked midway at Tiruchirappalli, and a few more cultural personalities joined the yatra. On 21 April 1948, unmindful of the rush, the group travelled by the Shencottah passenger train and reached Tirunelveli at noon the following day.

The league met Chellamma Bharati and her daughter Thangammal at their Kailasapuram residence near the railway junction. Chellamma said she had no objection to her husband's works being nationalized. The league had carried T.S. Chockalingam's letter asking if she was

Bharati with family – wife, Chellamma; older daughter, Thangammal; and younger daughter, Shakuntala – and friends.

agreeable to the idea of nationalizing Bharati's works;* as we shall soon see, the respected journalist Chockalingam was Education Minister Avinashilingam's pointsman for non-official handling of the issue. Shanmugam states that on 23 April 1948 Chellamma gave a letter in the affirmative.

The following, according to Ediroli Viswanathan, is the text of Chellamma's letter.

Om

May Shakti bestow all blessings on the honourable Premier Ramaswamy Reddiar. I note that there is a public agitation going on in Tamilnadu to make Mahakavi Bharati's writings and poems public property. In this regard Narana Duraikannan, editor of *Prasanda Vikatan*, and A. Srinivasa Raghavan, editor of *Chintanai*, came to meet me. They state that the Madras Government is contemplating acquiring the

---

* This moving letter of consent is not to be found in government documents. However, a shorter letter written some ten months later, dated 14 February 1949, can be found along with one signed by her elder daughter, Thangammal. It is possible that the above letter was intended for Premier Reddiar's eyes while the latter was written at the instance of the Tirunelveli tahsildar in preparation for the government takeover of the copyright, and consequently found its way into the files.

rights to Bharati's writings from whosoever may have such rights and make them public property, and that you are showing sincere interest in this task. I greatly appreciate your magnanimity. I give full consent to the Government's efforts to acquire by fair means existing rights and future rights and make it over to the public. May your efforts succeed through the grace of Shakti. However, I hesitate to say this but cannot resist saying so. As you well know, the popularity of my husband's writings has yielded no special comforts to either myself or his family. I have the fullest confidence that you'll accomplish the present task in full conformity with the dictates of justice and fairness.

Even though Chellamma had given away all her rights, and as such had no locus standi legally speaking, her consent gave much legitimacy to the demand for nationalization. Given his stature and contribution to both the arts and nationalism, Shanmugam had considerable credibility. He worked in tandem with Bharati Viduthalai Kazhagam to conduct meetings across Tamilnadu in support of the demand. In government files we find resolutions passed by various organizations such as the Dindigul Town Congress Committee and the Salem Municipal Council calling for the nationalization of Bharati's works, indicating the widespread support the campaign was gathering.

~

Meanwhile, Meiyappan initiated legal proceedings. Apart from T.K.S. Bros., he sued Salem Shanmuga Films of Coimbatore, Ramanathan Pictures of Karaikudi, Sankar Pictures of Srirangam and Jaya Films of Salem, all involved in the production of *Bilhanan*.

Meiyappan filed an interlocutory application in the district court of Coimbatore to prevent screening until disposal of the suit. He filed twenty-three documents, including copies of the copyright assignment made by Chellamma to Bharati Prachuralayam, the deed signed between Bharati Prachuralayam and Jeshinglal Mehta, the assignment made by Jeshinglal Mehta to Meiyappan, apart from documents from AIR, Travancore and Mysore radios recognizing Meiyappan's broadcast rights.

For his part, Shanmugam could produce only press clippings and the claim that oral permission from Nellaiyappa Pillai, friend and publisher of Bharati, had been received. He also raised the issue that since Bharati lived in the French territory of Pondicherry, British law may not be valid. The only substantive point raised was on ethical and moral grounds that the songs of Bharati should be deemed 'to be public property and not the property of any individual'. 'The literary works of [Bharati] are not such as would be governed by the ordinary rules and provision of copyright,' he claimed. Despite the legal weakness of the defence, the district judge B. Koman dismissed the interlocutory application on 16 April 1948; he stated that the loss, if any, could be easily ascertained as the contentious portion of the film was about 90–250 feet only and therefore the remedy lay in awarding damages and not in stopping the screening of the film.

Government Takes Note

As the campaign for nationalizing Bharati's works gathered steam, the government of Madras state, in a newly independent country, had to reckon with it. Given Shanmugam's association with the freedom struggle and proximity to political personalities, he had taken the battle to the government. He wrote two letters, one to Premier Ramaswamy Reddiar and the other to Dr T.S.S. Rajan, an associate of V.V.S. Aiyar and V.D. Savarkar during their London days, a prominent Congressman, a trusted associate of Rajaji and minister of food and public health in Ramaswamy Reddiar's cabinet. The latter letter was immediately passed on to Education

Minister T.S. Avinashilingam. That Ramaswamy Reddiar and Avinashilingam were at the helm of affairs when the demand was raised was indeed fortuitous. But for these men of impeccable honesty and exemplary resourcefulness, the issue might not have panned out the way it did. Who were these men?

The Peasant Premier

Omandur P. Ramaswamy Reddiar was the first premier of Madras province who did not have a college degree or even much formal education. In early 1947, when Rajaji and K. Kamaraj factions of the Congress party in Madras decided it was time to dethrone the incumbent premier T. Prakasam, they could find no one better than Ramaswamy Reddiar to take his place. Ramaswamy Reddiar was not a man to seek office but when it came knocking at his door, he was not one to forsake it either. From March 1947, until he gave up office a little over two years later, Ramaswamy Reddiar was far from being a popular leader – most certainly not with his fellow legislators – but was surely the most feared for his excessive honesty and probity in public life.

Ramaswamy Reddiar's two years as premier of Madras were eventful. He had the privilege of unfurling the Indian flag at Fort St George on India's midnight tryst with destiny. The aftermath of Gandhi's assassination passed without any untoward incident in the province, largely due to his deft handling. Prohibition, first introduced in Salem district in 1937, was extended to the whole of the province. Though the first years of independence were marked by the failure of monsoon, resulting in drought and acute public discontent, he ably handled not only the food scarcity but also the strikes by government employees and labourers. The hated and exploitative zamindari system was also abolished during his time. He showed great alacrity in readying forces during the Hyderabad crisis when its Nizam refused to accede to the Indian Union. To these achievements should be added the nationalization of Bharati.

Born in 1895 in Omandur, 10 km from Tindivanam on the road to Pondicherry, Ramaswamy Reddiar studied only up to class eight. Chandrasekara Saraswathi, the later head of the Kanchi Mutt, was his schoolmate.

Despite the lack of proper schooling, Ramaswamy Reddiar was well read and had a working knowledge of English, and easily held his own among Indian Civil Service (ICS) bureaucrats and in the legislature. Once when he was asked for an opinion on some matter by the central government, he got the spelling of the word 'opinion' wrong in his written note. When his ICS secretary wanted to correct it, Ramaswamy Reddiar bluntly told him that Nehru preferred to have his opinion rather than find out if he knew its spelling.

Ramaswamy Reddiar married in 1916, and his wife died four years later. His only son, Sundaram, died in 1927, and an already spiritually inclined Ramaswamy Reddiar devoted all his energies to public life.

A hardy peasant, his farm produce was legendary for its quality. Appropriately enough, the biography of this rustic man is titled *Vivasaya Mudalamaichar* (The Peasant Premier). Nehru described him as 'an uncut diamond'.

Gandhian politics attracted him; he joined the Non-Cooperation Movement in 1919 and attended the special session of the Congress at Nagpur the next year. In 1930 he joined the Salt Satyagraha and was arrested on the march towards Vedaranyam. A spell of prison for involvement in the Civil Disobedience Movement followed. Deeply involved in the Khadi Movement – as can be expected, he wore only khadi all his life – he picketed shops selling foreign cloth. He joined the Individual Satyagraha and the Quit India Movement, and was imprisoned on both occasions. He turned his native district of South Arcot, once the citadel of the rival Justice Party, into a bastion of the Congress party. In the intra-party struggles in the Congress, he took a bold position against Rajaji.

A short-tempered man, he had little patience for people he did not trust. His stubbornness in dealing with party men, including legislators, made him hugely unpopular within the party. When he was once invited to preside over a function to pay homage to V.O. Chidambaram Pillai, he gruffly declined saying that he had pressing administrative duties that were more important than commemorating the life of patriots.

Another sticking point was the alleged anti-Brahmin prejudice of this devotee of Ramana Maharshi – a stick that was used to ultimately hound Ramaswamy Reddiar out of office. In April 1949 he resigned from the premiership with his head held high, immediately vacated the official residence, Cooum House, and proceeded to his village the very next day, where he lived until his death twenty-two years later in 1970.

That a man of his morality and resolve was the head of the government certainly helped the cause of nationalizing Bharati's writings. That he had a trusted lieutenant in Avinashilingam, whose honesty and integrity, if anything, were only superior to his premier's, greatly aided the cause.

The Gandhian Educationist

Tiruppur Subramaniam Avinashilingam Chettiar was born in 1903 in Tiruppur. Barely 40 km east of

Coimbatore, Tiruppur was then a sleepy town, a far cry from the hosiery capital it is now. Avinashilingam's father was a successful merchant and banker, while his mother was a religious woman. He was one of four brothers and four sisters, and the entire family was known for its philanthropy. Avinashilingam was filled with happiness whenever he saw the choultries (free inns for travellers and pilgrims) endowed by his forefathers dotting the Coimbatore region.

After schooling in Coimbatore, Avinashilingam studied at Pachaiyappa's College in Chennai and then pursued law. His roommate there, Chinnu, who later became Swami Chidbhavananda, remained his lifelong friend. It was through him that he met two direct disciples of Ramakrishna Paramahamsa: Brahmananda and Shivananda. Avinashilingam and Chinnu trudged to the local Ramakrishna Mutt every day for six months to meet Shivananda. Visiting Belur Mutt, the headquarters of the Ramakrishna Mission, near Calcutta, soon became an annual ritual for Avinashilingam. On one such visit he met Mahendranath Gupta, popularly known as M, the celebrated chronicler of the Gospel of Sri Ramakrishna.

Avinashilingam apprenticed as a lawyer but after a few years he lost interest in the profession. In 1930 he stared an orphanage and school which would soon grow into the Ramakrishna Vidyalaya, and branch into various institutions of higher education through the century. The first student he admitted was a Dalit boy, an act that triggered social boycott of the school. Avinashilingam held his ground, and through tactical material enticements such as free food, clothing and books he drew poor students from all castes.

Shortly after establishing this school, circumstances forced Avinashilingam to plunge into direct political activity. As a student in Chennai he attended the massive Satyagraha meeting on Marina Beach in 1920. The image of a puny Gandhi beside the gigantic figure of Shaukat Ali would remain etched in his mind. Avinashilingam met Gandhi in Tiruppur in 1926 when the latter was on an all-India tour as part of the Khadi Movement. Not surprisingly for a young man of his idealism, Avinashilingam was soon caught in Gandhi's web and learnt valuable lessons in public life.

In April 1930, when news of police brutality on the peaceful Dandi Salt Satyagraha volunteers and the arrest of Gandhi reached him, Avinashilingam could not resist breaking the salt laws himself. Promptly arrested, he was sentenced to six months of rigorous imprisonment including a spell of demoralizing solitary confinement. Two years later he was again imprisoned for a year for participating in the Civil Disobedience Movement. Two more spells of imprisonment were to follow – in 1941, as part of the Individual Satyagraha and then again during the Quit India Movement, just like Ramaswamy Reddiar. Avinashilingam's imprisonments deeply saddened his family and hastened his father's death. It was a sadness accentuated by his commitment to celibacy and refusal to marry.

Avinashilingam was elected to the Central Assembly in 1935, humbling the heavyweight R.K. Shanmugam Chettiar, who later became the first finance minister of independent India. Shanmugam Chettiar was touched by the thirty-two-year-old man's humility and sincerity, when, despite being victorious, Avinashilingam visited him in his home to seek his advice.

Avinashilingam's time in prison facilitated the forging of many lifelong friendships among fellow nationalists. It also gave him the time and solitude for a thorough reading of ethical and religious texts, including the *Tirukkural*, Kamban's *Ramayanam* and the writings of Vivekananda. He translated Vivekananda's *Lectures from Colombo to Almora* into Tamil.

In 1946 Avinashilingam established the Tamil Academy, an organization for the development of the Tamil language. On the eve of India's independence, he announced his ambitious plan for producing an encyclopedia in Tamil, the very first in any Indian language. By this time he had been elected to the state assembly and was made minister of education. Single-handedly, he not only raised the huge sum of money required for the project but also, more importantly, put together a team of scholars to execute the work. By 1963, fifteen years after the first announcement, nine volumes totalling some 7000 pages were published, and five years later, a supplementary volume complete with an index was out. This was followed by a children's encyclopedia with multicoloured pages, another Indian-language first. Avinashilingam also oversaw the translation and publication of Gandhi's collected works in Tamil in seventeen volumes under the aegis of the Gandhi Smarak Nidhi.

Despite being reviled by the Dravidian Movement for his support of Hindi, Avinashilingam's contribution to the development of the Tamil language is unparalleled. As education minister, he enhanced budgetary allocation for schools, brought pay parity to Tamil teachers, and generally made life better for all teachers. (Referring to the antediluvian nature of Tamil-language teachers, he once famously said that they did not even know how to switch on an electric light.) Known for his scrupulous honesty, Avinashilingam was a tough taskmaster who would not rest until the goal had been achieved.

Avinashilingam proved to be a perfect foil for Ramaswamy Reddiar, and the two in tandem soon steered the nationalization issue successfully.

Government Swings into Action

In the two letters Shanmugam wrote to the premier and a minister, we find two marginal notes in the premier's own hand. The first is addressed to the law department: 'Secretary legal may see and explain position. O.P.R. 7-4[-1948].' On the letter to T.S.S. Rajan, a day after, we find an equally cryptic, 'H[onourable]. M[inister]. Education may see and kindly make arrangements to acquire copyright. O.P.R. 8-4[-1948]'.

In a matter of a day the premier had instructed Education Minister Avinashilingam to handle the issue, from merely exploring the possibility of acquiring the copyright to making a decision on government takeover. Quite understandable, since the Congress was committed to Bharati and well knew the emotional appeal the issue possessed in the popular imagination.

The wheels of the government turn but slowly. This was especially true for the new government in independent India which was a stickler for procedures and formalities. It ultimately took about a year for the intent of Ramaswamy Reddiar's marginal note to be translated as a pronouncement on the floor of the Legislative Assembly.

As soon as the task was entrusted to him, Avinashilingam took it on in earnest. When he asked in a note to the premier 'If the cabinet will give me the power to negotiate over the matter', he meant business. On the same day, Ramaswamy Reddiar approved the note of his trusted minister: 'H[onourable] M[inister] Education is requested to make arrangements with Bharathi's relations to make Bharathi's songs to the public.'

Public mood was at the top of Avinashilingam's mind, and he demanded quick bureaucratic action. In his note to the secretary of law department on 8 April 1948, Avinashilingam pointed out: 'There is a great deal of agitation that Bharati's works must be made free for everybody to utilize. The legal position of these rights may be examined and it may also be considered whether we cannot acquire those rights under law.'

When the education department, in its own routine manner, sought to ask the Director of Public Instruction (DPI) about this issue, Avinashilingam interjected swiftly (3 May 1948), 'I am afraid the note of the DPI will not produce any light,' and emphasized that 'The point is what is the legal position today ... the present position may be examined legally and steps taken to get it acquired as a public property'. (Avinashilingam was quite right. When the DPI finally presented its note following a reminder, on 4 May 1948, after consulting the Registrar of Books, it produced no earth-shattering information. After the Copyright Act, 1914 had been introduced, the practice of registering copyright had ceased and the only information the note produced was the already well-known fact that it was Bharati Prachuralayam which owned the copyright.)

Soon Avinashilingam also decided that the matter would be deliberated upon confidentially.

Meanwhile, in an effort to speed up things, and knowing the hidebound ways in which officialdom thought and worked, Avinashilingam asked his friend T.S. Chockalingam to seek legal opinion on the issue. The legal opinion of Dr A. Krishnaswami, a barrister, came in a week: 'Prima facie it appears that the legal representatives of the original owner can exercise full rights after expiry of 25 years of the poet and till the expiry of the aggregate of 50 years, after which it becomes public property.'

Meanwhile, the government also asked the district administration of Coimbatore to report on the infringement of copyright case between Meiyappan and Shanmugam as it had implications for the government acquiring copyright. ('The Collector is requested to treat the matter AS SPECIAL and send his report immediately.') Shanmugam aided the effort and sent all the documents that he had collected to Avinashilingam.

But the days rolled by without progress. Despite the policy decision to acquire the copyright, the procedural delays began to exacerbate Avinashilingam's impatience. He observed in a note (19 May 1948) to the education secretary: 'There is a great deal of agitation in the matter and the sooner we acquire it the better. If we delay it unnecessarily, we have to yield to public agitation. I expect the matter to be examined and put up within a week.'

~

The public mood favoured an early resolution that would support the free use of Bharati's work. And even as Meiyappan conceded, the agitation had by then become broad-based and credible with the 'interested parties [having] been able by some specious reasoning, to get as their supporters some gentlemen whose patriotism, disinterested motives and bona fides are absolutely above question'. In fact, the primary reason for the success of the agitation was the credibility of those in the forefront of the movement, the genuineness of their demand and the all-round popular support that they could mobilize.

The agitation that Avinashilingam was referring to targeted two persons – first, Meiyappan, and secondly, Visvanathan. Despite being only a secondary target – for the case pertained only to recording rights and not publishing rights – Visvanathan too felt the heat. As he recalled a year later, 'I was looked upon as public enemy no. 1 and treated as such on many a platform and in the press. I was likened to a monster, growing fat on the sale proceeds of Bharati's works all by myself.' It even made him wonder, 'is the charge of monopoly and profiteering tenable?' On the other hand, Meiyappan was seen for what he was, a shrewd businessman and capitalist out to make money in the film industry.

Realizing that the 'matter ... has been, now and again, a subject of discussion in some circles in Tamilnadu', and it was a matter in which 'public interest ... may be said to be involved', Meiyappan tried to deflect the attention. Towards this end he submitted a long missive to the premier on 2 June 1948. Claiming that all his films provided 'popular entertainment compatible with perfect cleanliness and high quality art in production ... to which no exception can be taken by the most fastidious critics', he even offered to screen these films especially for the premier and other members of the government; Meiyappan did not realize that if Gandhi had watched at least one film in his life, his diehard disciple Ramaswamy Reddiar had never seen any. His acquisition of the broadcast rights of Bharati's works, Meiyappan contended, was purely 'in pursuance of my plan of combining moral purpose and instructional value with entertainment'. Meiyappan also claimed that he had made some of Bharati's songs 'a household word in Tamilnadu' after spending 'very considerable time, labour and research'. In his defence on holding the rights,

Meiyappan asserted that to get 'the best possible benefits', the songs should be sung only by '"high"-class artists in a proper manner'.

> The ownership of exclusive rights by me has so far helped to maintain the quality of the songs sung at a very high level of excellence. I have allowed, in regard to gramophone recording, musical pieces sung only by such top quality artistes as Srimati M.S. Subbalakshmi, Srimati D.K. Pattammal and Sri T.R. Mahalingam.

Meiyappan added that though Bharati's songs should be sung by the masses, all the same it was necessary that 'the patterns of singing them must be unexceptionable'. He further pointed out that the fact of his having given permission gratis to AIR, Travancore and Mysore radios proved his bona fide intent and demonstrated his willingness to serve the public cause. Why then did he not let other film-makers use Bharati's songs? Meiyappan adduced a reason for this.

In the case 'of film producers and gramophone recording concerns, I feel that the position is different. Their primary aim is utilizing Bharathi's songs . . . [it] is not public service, but is exploitation for commercial purposes of the public good will [and] popularity'. This distinction between 'those who value art for its own sake and those who exploit it for commercial purposes', he claimed, had been 'misrepresented by some interested parties as ... "imprisoning Bharathiar's soul and works"'. In such a situation where 'the interested persons are wanting to develop the controversy and misrepresent the facts for their own ulterior purposes', attempted solutions were becoming 'infructuous'. Therefore, he had approached the government and was making a proposal.

Meiyappan offered to assign his copyright as a gift to a trust which would be composed of himself (or his nominee) and two or more government nominees. Requests to use Bharati's works, he suggested, could be made to this trust, which would finalize the terms. As for his own use, he requested that permission be given as a matter of routine and without payment.

Clearly, public pressure was on Meiyappan and he did not want to draw either public displeasure or government disapproval. In fact, he was making a virtue out of a necessity. But what he was offering was too complicated and came too late in the day for the government to consider seriously.

Meanwhile, Avinashilingam, acutely conscious of public pressure, was even considering, 'whether [copyright] could be acquired through court, if private negotiation fails' [note dated 7 June 1948]. But with the broadcast rights being sub judice, his hands were tied.

Who Owns That Song?

Avinashilingam repeatedly pointed out to his cabinet colleagues and officials that 'I must also say that the people are restive over the matter and there is a general demand from the public that Bharathi's works must be made public property and so, I feel that urgent action must be taken as soon as possible without waiting for the decision of the courts' (note dated 4 August 1948). But the premier, who wanted to play by the book, tended not to concur. 'However make arrangements to purchase as soon as the court desides,' the premier noted on 5 August 1948.

~

Meanwhile, the proceedings in the court had begun. An earlier interlocutory application to prevent the screening of *Bilhanan* until the disposal of the suit, as noted earlier, had been dismissed by the court on the ground that if copyright infringement was proved then the remedy would be to seek damages.

The full hearing on Original Suit No. 4 of 1948 came up soon. Meiyappan stated that he was using the same song, '*Thoondil puzhuvinai pol...*' in his own film, *Vedhala Ulagam*, which was under production. Shanmugam's contention that Bharati's works were public property was 'a frivolous and untenable plea', he argued. He prayed for a perpetual injunction against the use of this and other Bharati songs, and claimed damages worth Rs 11,000, a climbdown from the initially threatened Rs 50,000.

Shanmugam, the first defendant, in his written statement declared that 'The deceased Subramania Bharathi was such an eminent Tamil poet, that his literary works became dedicated to the public and they became the property of the public in Tamil Nad. The literary works of the said poet are not such as would be governed by the ordinary rules and provisions of copyright.' He also, implausibly, argued that Bharati had bequeathed his entire copyright to Nellaiyappa Pillai through an 'oral will'.

In challenging the assignment deed signed between Jeshinglal Mehta and Meiyappan, Shanmugam charged that 'The nominally and colourable nature of the document would be evidenced from the fact that the plaintiff has chosen to hurry up and have the document executed on the last day of the expiry of the period of the 25th year from the date of the death of the poet'.

Shanmugam further contended that he had already used Bharati's song in praise of the Tamil language in *Menaka*, made in 1935, and neither Jeshinglal Mehta nor Meiyappan had objected then. Similarly, in his 1941 film *Gumastavin Penn* he had used not one but four poems of Bharati, once again with no objection being raised. He therefore contended that 'It is strange and extraordinary that the Plaintiff should choose to state that the defendant has made an infringement of the alleged copyright of the plaintiff in the literary works of the poet, by making records of only 12 lines among the thousands and thousands of lines of the poems of the poet.'

~

In continuing to resolve the issue, the government worked through the government pleader in Coimbatore to confidentially obtain certified copies of the plaint and various other documents. The government also corresponded with Meiyappan in late August 1948 to acquire copies of documents that would prove his ownership of copyright. Meiyappan promptly obliged by sending copies.

On the education department's request to examine the suit, with the permission of the district judge, the government pleader at Coimbatore was of the view that since Bharati Prachuralayam had only assigned partial rights to Jeshinglal Mehta, Meiyappan held only those rights. He also held Shanmugam's plea of Bharati's writings not being the property of any individual as 'not sustainable'. In his view, therefore, if the government was to acquire copyright of all works, it would have to do so from both Bharati Prachuralayam and Meiyappan. This was indeed a significant legal point.

Based on these two sets of documents, the views of Government Solicitor H.M. Small were sought. In a note dated 9 November 1948, Small averred that 'a detailed enquiry should first be made into the history of the publication . . . with reference to time and place of publication' and if copyright still 'subsisted in any person or persons', all copyright holders and assignees 'may join in one deed of assignment in favour of Govt'. This opinion was in consonance with the government pleader's view that all the stakeholders involved should come together and hand over the copyright.

Following the government solicitor's advice, the education department, in a confidential memorandum dated 10 January 1949, stated that 'The Government have under consideration a proposal to acquire the copyright in the late poet Subramania Bharathi's works in order that the songs of the Poet can be made available to the public at large'. Towards this end it instructed the collector of Tirunelveli to collect all information on the history of the publication of Bharati's works. With this instruction the government machinery began to work swiftly, and the process of nationalization picked up speed.

Meanwhile, Avinashilingam met Thangammal (it is not clear if he met Chellamma also; both mother and daughter lived together) on a tour of Tirunelveli district. Thangammal, apart from seeking some provision for her maintenance, reminded him that the court case pertained only to broadcast rights and, therefore, the government should immediately proceed with acquiring publication rights from Visvanathan. An unsavoury desire to deprive Visvanathan of his rights can be sensed in this demand. This was born perhaps either out of a post facto feeling that the family had been short-changed when the copyright changed hands or that her uncle was making considerable money when her own family was in dire financial difficulties. The hostility of the Bharati family towards Visvanathan is also evidenced by the fact that Chellamma's biography of Bharati written a few years earlier in 1944, though replete with family details, contains no reference at all to Visvanathan.

As instructed by the government, the tahsildar of Tirunelveli sought detailed accounts of the publication and transfer of copyright from Chellamma Bharati and Thangammal Bharati, as well as R. Sambasiva Iyer, Bharati's maternal uncle. Avinashilingam's meeting with Thangammal was a definite catalyst in the process, and also made him resolve to materially support the Bharati family.

Make it Public!

On 5 February 1949 Chellamma and Thangammal submitted a detailed account which was sent to Avinashilingam with a covering letter. This narrative is an important and interesting document. Chellamma presented a list of nine works published from Pondicherry by Bharati during his exile, and stated that 'neither he nor any one of us have assigned copyright over these works to anyone in Pondicherry or in [British] India. All these books were published by Bharati himself at his own expense, and therefore the copyright vests only' with the family. While Chellamma conceded that she had sold, for a sum of Rs 4000, the copyright to most of Bharati's works to Bharati Prachuralayam in 1931, she argued that the rights to *Aaril Oru Pangu, Kanavu* and *The Fox with the Golden Tail* continued to be vested in her. This is, to say the least, confusing but perhaps indicates that the legal transfer of the copyright was anything but straightforward and simple.

Bharati's younger daughter, Shakuntala, lived in Brunei, North Borneo, at that time, with her husband and, therefore, no statement was sought or received from her.

Sambasiva Iyer, though a brother of Bharati's mother, was only three years older than the poet, and had been his playmate in his boyhood. Incidentally, he still lived in Ettayapuram. He did not know much about the case, and stated that all details may be had from Visvanathan who had made the effort to gather Bharati's publications and manuscripts from various sources. That he made no mention of Chellamma and her daughters in relation to the matter of copyright perhaps indicates that the Bharati family was divided over the matter.

Now that the government had a clear idea, after these consultations, of the publication history of Bharati's works and had cut through the legal morass of its ownership, the pace of the acquisition quickened.

One day, in the first week of March 1949, at seven in the evening, a motorcycle-borne messenger arrived at Meiyappan's house and delivered a 'very urgent' message: he was asked to meet the premier in an hour's time. Meiyappan hurried to Ramaswamy Reddiar's official residence, the Cooum House in the Government Estate. The rustic premier, who was not known for niceties, came straight to the point. He said that the government had decided to make Bharati's works public property and asked that Meiyappan give up his rights. When Meiyappan responded that he had purchased the rights for Rs 10,000, the premier retorted that the government would compensate him adequately. 'Without a moment's thinking I replied that "I am willing to transfer my rights in Bharati's works to the government this very minute. I am prepared to make this transfer without any compensation. I do not seek even one rupee."'

Needless to say, the account provided by Meiyappan in his memoir is self-serving. He makes no mention at all of the fact that he had filed a suit to claim heavy damages, or that he had turned a deaf ear to the pleas of some of the most respected cultural figures of the time to release his stranglehold over Bharati's works, or that he had held out for more than a year.

Ramaswamy Reddiar's summons to Meiyappan to come in person was a determined move and was born out of the government's resolve to acquire the copyright. Though there is no official reference to this, we have Narana Duraikannan's contemporary testimony that the government, if required, was even ready to pass an ordinance to implement its decision. In a situation where the premier of the province had personally summoned him and made a demand couched as a request, Meiyappan had little leeway to manoeuvre. Deciding that humouring the government was the best option, he adroitly came forward to give up his rights gratis.

As a businessman in a new business known for its speculative nature, Meiyappan could scarcely risk the displeasure of the government, especially when he had only recently moved his studio from Karaikudi to Chennai. By giving up the broadcasting rights of Bharati's works, he transformed a potential liability into goodwill, an asset to his business house. That this move paid off, or rather continues to pay good dividends, is evidenced by the fact that, in the popular mind, it is Meiyappan's name that is associated with the nationalization of Bharati's works. His company AVM Studios continues to advertise this fact through its clients and well-wishers.

The Half-brother

Compared to Meiyappan, Visvanathan was on an entirely different footing. Unlike broadcast rights, which are virtual and intangible, Visvanathan's rights were material and concrete. How he had come to acquire the rights and executed the publication of Bharati's works has been outlined earlier.

Visvanathan was in fact the most unlikely candidate to be his half-brother's publisher. Born in December 1896, he was fourteen full years younger to his celebrated half-brother. Their father died when Visvanathan was an infant. The orphaned Bharati soon left for Varanasi to be raised by his aunt's family and did not return to Ettayapuram until early 1903. The twenty-one-year-old young man fresh from North India and bubbling with new and radical ideas may not have had much time for his six-year-old kid brother.

As Visvanathan recollected in a later interview, he spent only three short spells with Bharati. The first was in Chennai during the year before Bharati's exile to

Pondicherry in August 1908. Visvanathan lived with Bharati's family as a school student, first at Mylapore and later in the adjoining neighbourhood of Triplicane. After Bharati's exile to Pondicherry, Visvanathan studied at Ettayapuram until 1915, and subsequently spent a year at Tiruchirappalli completing his intermediate studies. Visvanathan was married when he was studying there, and the exiled Bharati could not have attended the wedding function. He graduated in History from American College, Madurai, spending three years (1917–20) there. During April–October 1919 Visvanathan was with Bharati after his return from Pondicherry and when he was desperately wooing the zamindar of Ettayapuram, and thereafter for a few months at Kadayam, Bharati's father-in-law's house.

During 1920–21 Visvanathan studied at Teachers' College in Chennai. Though the two lived separately – Visvanathan in Saidapet near his college with his mother and maternal uncle, and Bharati in Triplicane, some 10 km away – Visvanathan apparently visited Bharati's home every weekend. He was not in Chennai at the time of Bharati's death and, therefore, did not attend the funeral.

In 1922 Visvanathan became a schoolteacher in Manamadurai, a small town less than 50 km from Madurai on the road to Rameswaram. He retired as the headmaster of the school thirty-four years later, and died in Manamadurai, aged eighty-eight, in July 1984.

Given the circumstances outlined above, the relationship between the half-brothers is unlikely to have been close, especially considering the difference in age – almost a generation – and the fact that their life trajectories were entirely different with little more than tangential contact.

To be fair, in his long life, despite many opportunities to do otherwise, Visvanathan never claimed any special intimacy with Bharati, and maintained a certain dignity in his activities, even after he gave up his rights over Bharati's writings.

Only one letter exchanged between Bharati and Visvanathan has survived. Written by Bharati in August 1918, a few months before his Pondicherry exile ended, the letter is quite revealing.

> Reading your letter, I'm happy to note the level of your intellectual training.
>
> It is only right that you should look up to me for support, next only to our father. Due to a divine will I have not so far had the resources to sustain you. However, I hope in the very near future that good times will come and that I will acquire the capacity

to discharge my duties to people such as you ... Our sister, Lakshmi had some years ago ... asked for some money. I could not oblige her as I did not have any. Since then she hasn't written a word ... .

Do not write to me in English any more. Even if your Tamil is colloquial I'd be happy to read it. If you cannot write even in colloquial Tamil you may write in Sanskrit.

First is the acumen he demonstrates in spotting his half-brother's intellectual abilities – as we shall see, Visvanathan displayed considerable skill in editing Bharati's writings for publication. Even if he was no genius like his brother, his unpublished polemical statement at the time of the nationalization, quoted in this book at many places, attests to his writing skills. Bharati also draws attention to Visvanathan's poor Tamil. Ironically, this was the man who would ensure that Bharati's writings, most of which had not been put together between covers in his lifetime, were competently published and widely circulated. Bharati's confession that he had failed in his duties as the eldest son of the family is also poignant.

It was only through force of circumstance that Visvanathan became Bharati's publisher. As he recalled bitterly, 'I did not get [the copyright] as an heirloom, but acquired by hard cash in the midst of stress and strain.' He had first acquired publishing rights from his sister-in-law by advancing money, then formed a partnership firm with two others, and later became the sole proprietor of Bharati's copyright. It was under Visvanathan's stewardship that the bulk of Bharati's writings were published, including a considerable volume of both unpublished and uncollected writings.

The increasing popularity of Bharati's writings between the 1920s and 1940s was predicated on the books made available by Visvanathan and Bharati Prachuralayam. In the prevailing mood of an ascendant nationalism and the rise of literary modernism, Bharati was an essential ingredient. Bharati Prachuralayam's success evoked criticism – both justified and unjustified – in its wake.

In an insightful reflection of the state of Tamil publishing, Bharati had commented in 1916:

> The state of authors in Tamilnadu continues to be precarious. Because entrepreneurs who will take up publishing as a business have not yet emerged, there is still some difficulty [for Tamil authors] . . . Surprisingly, our entrepreneurs have not taken sufficient interest in [book publishing]. Books are, of course, being published now. And a vast number of people do indeed buy and read them. If the book trade were systematically carried

out, people would have better books to choose from . . .
There is no doubt at all that good profits will accrue
from book publishing if it is pursued with enterprise.

Willy-nilly, it had fallen upon Visvanathan to realize Bharati's dream of making book publishing a commercially viable and successful enterprise. While Bharati's in-effect new books, both poetry and prose, were avidly consumed, Bharati Prachuralayam's editions were also criticized.

One criticism was that the publishing house functioned commercially with profit as its consideration. A particularly stark example of this criticism was the great short-story writer Pudumaippithan's comments on these editions. 'Talking of business immediately brings to mind Bharati Prachuralayam. Bharati Prachuralayam seems to think that there is no difference between Bharati and the textiles the Japanese are trying to dump on us.'

Apart from the aggressive or enterprising publishing that Visvanathan practised – one may choose the word according to one's predilections – there was a criticism that the texts swarmed with errors. Nellaiyappa Pillai is said to have been upset that sales were the prime concern for Bharati Prachuralayam, and that there was not a page without errors in their publications. Pudumaippithan also accused Bharati Prachuralayam of emending the text.

Scholars have debated and resolved these issues – largely in the publisher's favour – but such criticism is more an indication of the mood around Bharati Prachuralayam, among both Bharati's friends and critics. Bharati's associates perhaps saw Visvanathan as an upstart who could not claim his legacy. It is not the first time that business success has bred envy. This close monitoring of the efforts of Bharati Prachuralayam is also an index of the growing cultural importance of Bharati's writings as newer texts were being made available.

That not a penny went to Bharati's indigent wife and daughters when Bharati's books were doing good business added to the family's resentment. Few were willing to buy Visvanathan's defence: 'Fortunately both the sons-in-law of the poet were well settled in life and were earning both here and afterwards in the Malay states a fairly good income. This afforded the widow some comfort regarding her daughters, while she had not much to worry to keep the wolf from the door.'

And, therefore, though the primary target of the campaign for nationalizing Bharati was Meiyappan and the sole objective the free use of Bharati's songs on stage and cinema, as the campaign gained strength through 1948, shots aimed at Meiyappan also found their mark in Bharati Prachuralayam. As Visvanathan himself put it somewhat dramatically,

Make it Public!

> I was looked upon as public enemy no. 1 and treated as such on many a platform and in the press. I was likened to a monster, growing fat on the sale proceeds of Bharati's works all by myself. In the light of the facts stated above how is the charge of monopoly and profiteering tenable?

and wondered with self-pity,

> Is this the reward and recognition one gets for collecting, preserving and giving shape (the present classification of the works are all my own) to some of the greatest treasures the world has ever known? Are the accusers justified in equating me with those who must have made considerable money through the sales of the songs recorded in picture and plate?

Visvanathan was also cut up that the Bharati Viduthalai Kazhagam, which met Bharati's wife and daughter to seek their backing, did not so much as even make formal contact with him, not to speak of seeking his support.

Following legal advice, the government decided that the only way to proceed was to acquire all rights in one go. Meiyappan was the difficult customer, and once he had been tackled, it was rightly assumed that Visvanathan would simply comply. The ordinary schoolteacher and headmaster that he was, Visvanathan would not have the skill and savvy to negotiate with the all-powerful state.

The exact process by which Visvanathan was approached by the government is not evident in the record. Surely no motorcycle-borne special messenger carried summons, nor could his interaction with the government have been on an equal basis. Was he not merely the half-brother of a dead poet, eking out a living by teaching in a mofussil school?

Visvanathan did not have the wherewithal to give up his rights gratis to the government as Meiyappan had done, nor did his circumstances allow it. From the education minister's announcement, it is clear that while Meiyappan gave his consent letter on 11 March, Visvanathan's consent was acquired only the day after.

All the documents refer to correspondence with him only after the policy announcement on the floor of the assembly. They indicate that Visvanathan met the premier of the day and the education minister just before the announcement to convey his decision to transfer the copyright to the government.

In any case, Visvanathan agreed to a consideration of Rs 15,000 for transferring his rights. It is unlikely that he had any chance to negotiate the price; the official record is silent on this. If there were negotiations on this score it would surely have left a paper trail. Quite simply, the government had made an offer he could have had no say in. On the announcement of nationalization, Visvanathan stopped printing Bharati's books. A year and a half after selling the remaining stock under licence, he still had stock worth over Rs 20,000. Even a back-of-the-envelope calculation would indicate that Rs 15,000 was not adequate recompense.

A year later, Visvanathan would recall what had gone on in his mind at that time. He conceded that it was 'a good augury that in the changed atmosphere brought about by the attainment of Independence both the people and the Government have come forward to honour and encourage the writers of the new age'. Visvanathan had little doubt that the nationalization of Bharati amounted to 'recognition in a tangible form'. During the interview with the premier he had to make 'a great decision' in life that would make all the difference to his and his family's future. As he saw it there were two alternatives before him,

> whether, taking advantage of the fillip that is given to Bharati's works, to continue my business by giving effect to all my ideas of improved editions and make some money as any another man might do or to hand over to the state the works in the present complete and finished state and make what may be deemed a great sacrifice.

Who Owns That Song?

Visvanathan chose the second alternative. He claimed that better offers had been made to him in the previous five years or so, but he had refused to be tempted as he feared that the works would be utilized for purely mercenary ends. On this occasion, the offer had come from the government, 'the trustees of the nation'. Filled with 'the supreme satisfaction of having done my duty by the poet and making the works what they are at present', Visvanathan felt that there was no need to hold on to the rights any more. And there was no way he could have resisted the combined pressure of popular opinion and a determined government.

Not only did Visvanathan agree to this deal signed on 12 March 1949, in an unexpected move he came forward, of his own accord, to gift all the manuscripts of Bharati in his possession to the government so that they may be preserved in the government museum. A project that had occupied him for the better part of a quarter of a century, and in which he had invested considerable time, money and emotion, had suddenly been wrested out of his hands. It may not be wrong to surmise that his decision to gift the manuscripts was out of pique, to demonstrate his displeasure about the decision and the way it had been enforced.

Make it Public!

The government's negotiations with Visvanathan and Meiyappan probably took place in the second week of March 1949. As the deal was concluded to the satisfaction of the government, Avinashilingam made the momentous announcement on the floor of the legislature on 12 March. To the resounding thumping of desks by the members of the house he declared:

> There is a popular feeling that the works of Sri C. Subramania Bharati, the great poet of Modern Tamil Renaissance, should be acquired by the Government and made available for the use of the public generally at as cheap a cost as possible. I have great pleasure in informing this House, and through the House, the public at large, that Sri A.V. Meiyappa Chettiar has agreed to convey to the Government the rights vested in him of reproducing the Poet's songs by sound reproducing or broadcasting devices ...
>
> Sri C. Visvanatha Iyer, the Poet's brother, has also agreed to convey to the Government his proprietary rights in regard to the printing and publication of the poet's works to the Government for a consideration of Rs 15,000. In addition, he has agreed to convey as a gift the manuscripts of the poet in order that they may be kept in a befitting manner in the Government Museum ...

The Government wish to convey their thanks to Sri A.V. Meiyappa Chettiar for his gift and to Sri Visvanatha Iyer for his gift of the Poet's manuscripts and for agreeing to convey his publishing rights. The Government will make such arrangements as they think fit to make the poet's work popular and available to the public at as cheap a cost as possible.

With this announcement the campaign to nationalize Bharati's works came to a fruitful end after a little over a year, marking a unique moment in modern literary history when the state acquired the copyright of an author.

4

Nationalization and After

Compensating the Family

Amid the tortuous process of nationalizing Bharati and the flurry of activity, Avinashilingam had not forgotten Thangammal's request to 'make some provision for her own maintenance'. Even as negotiations were on with Meiyappan and Visvanathan, Avinashilingam requested sanction 'to purchase such rights as the wife and the two daughters of the poet [may possess] or to give them as a gift' and asked for a sum of Rs 5000 for Chellamma and Rs 5000 each for the two daughters. He also sought 'urgent procedures' for the sanction and release of this amount. This note was written on 11 March 1949, the same date on which sanction for Visvanathan was being discussed. Avinashilingam's note was approved the very next day by both the finance minister and the premier.

This demonstrates Avinashilingam's commitment and concern for Bharati's family. Having alienated themselves from all rights over Bharati's works, Bharati's wife and daughters had little grounds for expecting any compensation. Avinashilingam was moved by ethical considerations and moral compulsions in getting approval for this amount – equal to the consideration paid to Visvanathan for relinquishing the entire publishing rights.

The note seeking sanction is carefully worded: Avinashilingam sought this amount either as a consideration of the 'purchase of such rights' or 'to give them as a gift'. Over a month later he reiterated this in another note: 'if they have no right, we may give them the amount as a gift'.

While this was indeed a magnanimous gesture on the part of the government, that it was passed by the hawk-eyed bureaucrats of the finance department can be interpreted as a pre-emptive move to cover any residuary rights that the family could be holding. In keeping with this understanding, before releasing the amount, the district collector of Tirunelveli was instructed to get a written undertaking from both Chellamma and Thangammal conveying all and any rights they may be holding to the works of Bharati. Accordingly, such an undertaking was provided by the two on 1 May – nearly two months after the sanction, after which the promised money was released to them. So much for the 'urgent procedure' that Avinashilingam had sought.

As Shakuntala was in Brunei, there was a delay of a few months in remitting the gratuity to her. On 21 July 1949 she wrote to Agriculture Minister M. Bhaktavatsalam requesting that the money be deposited in her account in the T. Nagar branch of the Indian Bank. Why she wrote to the agriculture minister is not clear. On 18 October 1949 she too signed an undertaking identical to the one given by her mother and sister.

Unfinished Business: Tagore Translated

The public announcement also led one other claimant of copyright over Bharati's stray works to approach the government.

Mandayam S. Srinivasacharya (1876–1968), or Sri Sri Acharya, belonged to the famed Mandayam family. Srinivasacharya's elder brother S. Thirumalacharya owned *Vijaya*, the daily that Bharati edited from Pondicherry. Srinivasacharya himself was the publisher and proprietor of the weekly *India* that Bharati edited when it was shifted lock, stock and barrel to

Pondicherry. *India* was founded by Srinivasacharya's cousin S.N. Thirumalacharya. Mandayam Alasinga Perumal, who belonged to the same family, proposed the idea of hiring Bharati for *India*. He had been a key figure in raising funds for Swami Vivekananda's historic trip to the World Congress of Religions at Chicago (1893). Srinivasacharya's nephew Mandayam Prativadi Thirumalacharya or M.P.T. Acharya (1887–1954), also involved in managing *India*, had a colourful life and was part of the India House group in London that assassinated the British official Lord Curzon Wyllie in July 1909. M.P.T. Acharya was a founding member of the CPI when it was established in Tashkent in 1920. His political career suffered a major setback when he fell out with M.N. Roy; he became an anarcho-syndicalist, and was an émigré in Berlin before he finally returned to India and died in poverty. Srinivasacharya's younger brother S. Parthasarathy canvassed shares from all over India for the Swadeshi Steam Navigation Company, especially when it was in the doldrums after V.O. Chidambaram Pillai's imprisonment.

Srinivasacharya, unlike Bharati, was socially conservative but he and Bharati shared the same political views. During the long years of exile in Pondicherry the two became especially close, and in the face of so many shared adversities their families bonded too. Bharati was very fond of Srinivasacharya's daughter Yadugiri, and she would go on to pen a celebrated memoir of her association with Bharati.

A man of considerable means, Srinivasacharya invested heavily in the Swadeshi Steam Navigation Company and the nationalist papers, and consequently lost a lot of money, banking on their success. He was under the close watch of the police and spies in Pondicherry for being a Swadeshi nationalist. It was he who found a house for Aurobindo when he first arrived in Pondicherry.

Less than two weeks after the government announced Bharati's nationalization, Avinashilingam received a letter in English from Srinivasacharya. Learning that the government was planning to nationalize all of Bharati's works, Srinivasacharya wrote that he had published in book form Bharati's translation of eight short stories by Rabindranath Tagore, towards the end of Bharati's exile in Pondicherry. He had paid for the translation, and thus held the copyright, he claimed. Wanting to know if the government would be 'willing to purchase the copyright', he also sought a personal interview with the education minister.

Bharati's interest in Tagore and his consequent attempt at translating him is a remarkable story, where a great poet unbeknown to another great poet followed his work and paid generous tribute.

Who Owns That Song?

Bharati was born twenty-one years after Rabindranath Tagore and predeceased Tagore by exactly twenty years. During his short life, Bharati demonstrated a remarkable engagement with Tagore and his writings – not only did he comment on Tagore's works frequently but also translated a considerable number of his essays and short stories.

The two poets never met. Bharati visited Calcutta in December 1906 for the annual session of the Congress but did not run into Tagore. Did he even know of Tagore and his writings at this point in time? Unlikely. More than a decade later, in early 1919, Tagore travelled to the south – to Madurai, Tiruchy, Thanjavur, Kumbakonam and Chennai. Bharati had been released from prison only a few months earlier; a broken man, he was still trying to find his feet in British India. By this time, Bharati had become more than familiar with Tagore's works. He was probably in Chennai when Tagore gave a talk at Gokhale Hall on 10 March, for Bharati himself had lectured not too far from there at the Victoria Public Hall about a week earlier. Tagore had come on a fundraising tour for Visva-Bharati at the instance of the Irish poet J.H. Cousins, who could claim some familiarity with Bharati's writings and had even translated a couple of Bharati's poems into English. The press gave Tagore's visit extensive coverage and it is impossible that Bharati could have missed it, but there is no record of him having had even a glimpse of Tagore. Given that Bharati was at this point being pre-censored by the police and was being shadowed, he might be condoned for having given Tagore a miss. If the two had met, it would have been worthy of record. Did Tagore, later in his life, come to know of Bharati's existence? That too remains unknown.

Between these two moments – Bharati's Calcutta visit in 1906 and Tagore's Chennai visit in 1919 – much water had flown under the bridge. This period, coinciding with Bharati's writing career, was marked by his engagement with the writings and reputation of Tagore.

A product of the Swadeshi Movement, Bharati was its perceptive chronicler and commentator, though unlike Tagore, he was not its critic. Bharati was up to his ears with the happenings in Bengal, commenting on and excerpting from Bengal journals. He translated Bankim's 'Bande Mataram' into Tamil (twice, actually). But, surprisingly and interestingly, there's no reference to Tagore at all during this time, between 1905 and 1911. One wonders what Bharati might have thought of Tagore's ambivalence towards the Swadeshi Movement after the Jamalpur riots (1907), considering that Bharati never saw the underbelly of nationalism. (We also don't know if Bharati had read and had an opinion on *The Home and the World*, a novel that illustrates Tagore's ambivalence about the movement.)

Bharati's first reference to Tagore is after the latter won the Nobel Prize in 1913. He invoked Tagore to express his opinion on Annie Besant's involvement in the freedom struggle. In response to an essay criticizing the nationalists for accepting Annie Besant's interventions in politics, Bharati wrote in *The Hindu* that this was fine so long as she did not involve herself in religious affairs and did not expect to become a leader of Indians in any regard. 'Intellectually and morally we have men in our land, and women, too, who cannot in the nature of things be dominated by her personality.' And what was the evidence on which Bharati asserted this? 'We produce men like Tagore and Bose nowadays.'

A correspondent of *The Hindu* who met Bharati in Pondicherry observed that given 'his manner of speaking emphasised as it is by tremendous thumping, sudden getting-up and sudden collapses' he 'remember[ed] nothing out of all his tirade, except his classification of Tilak as the first Indian statesman of the ages, of Prof. J.C. [Jagadish Chandra] Bose as the first scientist, and Rabindranath Tagore as the first Indian poet'.

Bharati's first real reference to Tagore comes in an essay written in November 1915. Narrating the now-familiar tale of ancient glory and medieval decline, Bharati saw the first rays of an Indian awakening during his time. 'We now see the signs of resurgence in everything. The Indian nation has been born anew. The whole world now acknowledges that Ravindranath is one of the mahakavis of our times.' The global acknowledgement of Tagore was a recurrent theme in Bharati's comments on Tagore.

Bharati translated into Tamil extracts from *The Crescent Moon*, a collection of poems and stories, and his joy in translating them is more than apparent. While these were prose translations, a year later he translated a Tagore poem on the glory of national education in four stanzas, from the same collection.

Bharati commented at length on Tagore's 1916 talk at the Imperial University of Tokyo and translated extensive passages from it. He saw Tagore's message as the awakening of a sleeping Asia by Japan. In his view, Tagore was only continuing Vivekananda's task. 'Vivekananda only revealed the exercise of the spirit. Tagore has now been sent by Mother India to show to the world that worldly life, true poetry and spiritual knowledge are rooted in the same dharma.' Assessing Tagore's credentials for this task, Bharati continues: '*Gitanjali* and the other books that he has translated and published in English are short. They are not extended epics or big plays. He revealed just a few lines of his lyrics. But the world was amazed.' In commenting on Tagore's global reception and his views on Asia's awakening, Bharati always returned to the literary genius of Tagore. He also expressed his dissatisfaction with the inadequate coverage given by Indian journals to Tagore's successful Japanese tour.

In 1918 Bharati was actively translating Tagore and published two books of his in Tamil. First came *Pancha Vyasangal*, a collection of five essays by Tagore originally published in the *Modern Review*. Shortly afterwards, Bharati's translations of eight stories from Tagore were published in a two-volume edition and included: 'False Hope', 'The Lost Jewels', 'Giribala', 'In the Middle of the Night', 'The Editor', 'Subha', 'The Homecoming' and 'The Conclusion'.

Given Bharati did not often translate any writer, that he translated so much of Tagore's works in itself can be seen as his worthy tribute to the Bengali poet. In translating Tagore, Bharati extensively annotated and added substantive footnotes.

Clearly Bharati keenly followed both Tagore's writings and activities. He invoked Tagore's name whenever he discussed the rise of the East, the resurgence of India and national education.

It is, therefore, a fitting poetic coincidence that Bharati's last published piece during his lifetime was on Tagore's successful European tour of 1921 and appropriately titled 'Sri Ravindra Digvijayam'.

> If one attains fame it should be like that of *mahan* [the great] Ravindrar. Is it only in Bengal? Is it just in India? Is it in Asia alone? His fame has spread across this earth from Germany to Austria to France. This despite his songs being written in Bengali. What the world has seen are only translations. And yet this fame!

In Bharati's view, however, the fame won by Tagore did not belong to him alone. 'Can the fame that is accumulated for one's own sake ever be called fame? Fame is that which comes from garnering glory for an entire nation. Ravindrar has established to the world that India is the *loka guru*. May the flowers at his feet be praised!'

Such fulsome and unconditional praise is yet to be heaped on one poet by another. For Bharati, Tagore's greatest achievement was fame, especially a fame that redounded to a fallen nation. A fame that he never experienced in his own lifetime. And did not know that he would gain posthumously.

~

It was the eight stories of Tagore translated and published by Bharati in 1918 that Srinivasacharya claimed the copyright for, and as proof indicated that these were not part of the volumes published by Bharati Prachuralayam.

On receipt of this letter, Avinashilingam wondered in a marginal note, 'I do not know how certain books of Bharati got into the hands of this individual.' A query was immediately sent to Visvanathan, who confirmed that Srinivasacharya's claim was true. Visvanathan added that he had acquired rights only from Bharati's heirs and not from others. On the question of whether the copyright should be acquired, Visvanathan said, 'It is left to the Government to negotiate independently if they care to purchase his right in Bharati's translations' or 'if it would be worthwhile purchasing this right'.

Taking Visvanathan's advice, the government responded to Srinivasacharya's letter in about three weeks' time – an indication of the earnestness with which Avinashilingam was handling the issue of Bharati's nationalization. Meanwhile, the DPI was sounded out on the idea, and he recommended the purchase of the copyright as he considered the book suitable for prescription as textbook for schools.

In August 1949 the government wrote to Srinivasacharya enquiring how much he would expect as compensation for selling his copyright for the translation. His reply was not direct.

Rather than merely quoting a figure, Srinivasacharya wrote a long letter. He began by stating that he had been the proprietor of *India* when Bharati edited it in his exile, and then described how he had facilitated Bharati's exile to Pondicherry. He also made the claim: 'Noticing his genius I left him free to develop it by his writings in my paper and by publishing his poems. Without any boast I may say that I discovered Bharathi and gave him full scope for the expression of his genius.' He drew attention to the help he had rendered to the poet 'from time to time in those dangerous and difficult days'. The veracity of this claim, he added, could be confirmed by writing to Sri Aurobindo. As can be imagined, this was the start of a long and painful story.

Srinivasacharya then detailed the heavy loss he suffered once the colonial government banned *India* and he was forced to scrap the printing press. Following this heavy loss, he met with a bigger calamity when the Swadeshi Steam Navigation Company failed and was liquidated. It was in such trying circumstances that he had asked Bharati to translate Tagore into Tamil. Given this background, he expected a tidy sum.

Srinivasacharya then provided a detailed estimate of the costs and revenue of publishing 3000 copies of the Tagore stories. Given these economics, and the fact that 'as a discoverer of Bharathi to India and as his helper and encourager and as being ruined in my two great national undertakings, it will not be much if I ask you Rs 10,000 for giving up my copyright', he wrote hopefully. He signed off his letter with:

> If the Government purchases my copyright for this amount it will be a fitting recognition of my humble services to the liberation of our motherland and to the development of our mother tongue through this great genius with whom I had the honour to live in close contact during the last twelve years of his life, almost as a member of a family.

Given that the government had paid Visvanathan only Rs 15,000 for the copyright for almost the whole lot of Bharati's writings, the DPI thought that Rs 10,000 'for a few translations appears to be exorbitant'.

But as one official commented, 'Government's policy [is] based on *sentiment*', and therefore the demand could not be easily dismissed. Another official too thought that the demand was 'preposterous' and was willing to offer only one-tenth of the sum. The education minister, somewhat more generous, thought 'we may pay a sum of Rs 2,500 and get it if he is agreeable'.

But Finance Minister B. Gopala Reddy took a tough stance: 'They are translations of Tagore's stories. Nothing is lost by not acquiring the copyright. We must stop this acquiring copyright business once for all.' By noting thus, the man known as 'Andhra Tagore' did not demonstrate good literary sensibility or appreciation for Bharati's importance. At least in this instance, he acted more like a finance minister.

The paper trail ends here, and it does not appear that the copyright of Bharati's translation of Tagore's stories was acquired by the government. Only in 1972, under the Copyright Act then in force, on the lapse of fifty calendar years after Bharati's death, did the translation fall into the public domain.

Executing the Transfer

The day after Meiyappan had gifted his rights to the government, he was sitting in the studio with some friends when Shanmugam and his brother Bhagavathy arrived with a big flower garland. The brothers had come to honour him for giving up his rights gratis. Meiyappan was reminded of an old poem about the anger of the noble amounting to drawing a line on a sheet of water while the fury of the depraved being engraved in stone.

A week later, at the well-known Hotel New Woodlands, Bharati Viduthalai Kazhagam threw a dinner to celebrate the triumph of the campaign. The function began appropriately with Shanmugam singing '*Jaya berigai kottada . . .*' (Let's beat the drum of victory . . .). Va.Ra.,

Who Owns That Song?

C.R. Srinivasan (editor of *Swadesamitran*), Parali S. Nellaiyappa Pillai, M.P. Sivagnanam, A. Srinivasa Raghavan and others participated in the event. Meiyappan was an honoured guest, and everyone felicitated him, including the Premier Ramaswamy Reddiar. It's not clear if Bharati's wife and daughter were invited to the dinner. Not only was Visvanathan not invited but certain statements and words uttered on the occasion are said to have wounded him, and the scars would remain with him until his death many decades later.

Despite some procedural delays, the transfer of Meiyappan's rights was a smooth process.

Once all the relevant documents had been filed at the Coimbatore court in the copyright infringement case against Shanmugam, Meiyappan informed the education secretary on 25 March 1949 that the handover of the documents would be somewhat delayed.

In agreeing to gift his broadcasting rights to the government, Meiyappan had committed to settling the suit out of court. Within a week the out-of-court settlement was concluded. In the Memorandum of Compromise dated 25 March 1949 submitted to the court, Meiyappan and Shanmugam agreed to the following: the defendants admitted the plaintiff's copyright and the plaintiff gave rights with retrospective effect to the defendants to use the Bharati song in contention; no further claims would be made on each other in relation to this dispute; both parties would bear their own costs; and the plaintiff would report the settlement to the court and withdraw the suit. This memorandum was filed in the court of Syed Imamuddin Sahib Bahadur on 11 April 1949, and the proceedings came to an end more than a year after Meiyappan had sent the first legal notice to Shanmugam.

Following this settlement, Meiyappan informed the education secretary on 2 June that he was now ready to sign the deed of transfer in favour of the government. On 8 June at the sub-registrar's office in Mylapore, he affixed his signature to the deed of absolute gift executed in favour of His Excellency the Governor of Madras. Though the deed was executed on 8 June the various clauses had retrospective effect from 12 March (the date of the declaration of state takeover of the copyright). The registration of the deed was exempted from stamp duty.

Visvanathan's Litany

Meiyappan's case was relatively easy as it was a simple deed of transfer of his rights as a gift. Once he had committed to signing, all he had to do was attend the celebration dinner.

In Visvanathan's case there were many issues to be handled. Bharati Prachuralayam held considerable unsold stock at the time of nationalization. Further, Visvanathan had offered to gift all of Bharati's manuscripts in his possession to the government for preservation in the government museum.

At the time of nationalization and the transfer of the rights, Visvanathan was in a sullen mood. In the background of the campaign in which he gave up his copyright, Visvanathan wrote in English a long polemical statement of nearly 5000 words. The immediate trigger was the dinner at New Woodlands on 17 March to celebrate 'the liberation of Poet Bharati from his erstwhile imprisonment'. Stung by 'the irresponsible speeches by some persons of note' at the dinner, he drafted a long statement.

Titled 'Service or Profiteering?', this cyclostyled statement was intended to be sent to the press and various public figures to clarify the charges against Visvanathan. But on the advice of friends and well-wishers that it might prejudice the government against him and harm his interests, he held it back. A year later he forwarded it to the government, which, not surprisingly, evinced no interest. In any case, given the lapse of time, what could have been an explosive bomb turned out to be a damp squib.

The statement shows that Bharati's creative genes were active in his half-brother. The avowed objective of the statement was 'to clear the wrong notions, wild conjecture and unjustified criticisms' levelled against Visvanathan.

The statement gave a detailed narrative of the posthumous publishing history of Bharati's works, the abortive attempts by Bharati's wife to publish his books, and how Visvanathan came to hold the copyright.

Visvanathan described the difficult conditions that necessitated the taking of a loan to meet the expenses of the marriage of Shakuntala, Bharati's second daughter. It was a time when 'None came forward either to purchase them or to help us in printing them.' Consequently, 'Our loan could not be discharged, nor a provision made for the poet's family.'

It was in this context that he had launched Bharati Prachuralayam with two other partners to publish Bharati's works exclusively. In 1931 Bharati Prachuralayam acquired the copyright for a sum of Rs 4000 to be paid in instalments. Visvanathan conceded: 'It is a low sum indeed, but considering the value of Bharati's works in those days, the offers that were made then and our own financial position, it was decent enough.' And as his partners left him one after another, he had to carry on his work single-handedly.

Only a part of Bharati's writings had been published in book form in his lifetime, and the rest were either in manuscript form or in files of paper cuttings in a highly damaged condition. A substantial part of his writings was scattered in various newspapers, and Visvanathan had to make special efforts to collect it. He had to spend a month in the Adyar Library (of the Theosophical Society's international headquarters in Chennai) to cull out the writings from Annie Besant's *New India* and *Commonweal*. He took the help of Sudhananda Bharati, then in the Aurobindo Ashram in Pondicherry, to gather the writings in *Arya*. Collecting the writings from the back volumes of *India* and *Swadesamitran* proved to be particularly challenging. He acquired the manuscript of the Bhagavad Gita translation from Vai.Su. Shanmugam Chettiar.

He had carried out the work of publication at a time, he asserted, when English was exalted and Tamil was looked down upon by the educated classes. The flip side of the political importance of Bharati's writings was the fact that

> the alien Government unleashed all its engines of repression, stifling, curbing and even annihilating everything that was national in character. That Bharati's works had their own share of victimization is part of the history of the period . . . they were banned. Our office was searched on several occasions, our files seized, our books confiscated. Personally, I was shadowed and my letters were intercepted and [I] was forbidden from entering Government Service. In the face of such

antagonism and harassment of the state I had not only to get on with the publications but also preserve such works as might be deemed objectionable by the Government.

And he wryly added, 'What was sedition in those days is political gospel today!'

Answering the charge that he had been raking in huge profits, Visvanathan asserted that he fixed a very low price for the books in keeping with Bharati's desire to 'make them available to the public as cheap as Japanese matches' and claimed that he had 'tried to fulfil the poet's wish to a considerable extent'. He also threw a challenge 'to the reading public to cite one instance in which a work resembling ours in bulk and value is given for so low a price'.

Regarding the reliability of the texts: 'I do not claim that our editions possess all that can be desired in the matter of publication. They can be improved considerably ... Of course there were many printers' mistakes in the early editions, which we rectified in subsequent ones.' In the case of 'different readings of the same lines', he asserted that 'they were given not without justification' and added that 'Bharati himself had these readings'.

Visvanathan was therefore pained that 'the people in Tamilnadu – the literate and the illiterate, the Congressmen and the Communist – ... joined in a campaign against me for the sin of possessing the copyright in the poet's works, which I did not get as an heirloom, but acquired by hard cash in the midst of stress and strain'.

Countering the claim that 'the works of a great poet are ... the asset of the nation', he asked, 'Have not Bharati's works become a national asset now in the truest sense?' He further asserted, 'There is nothing now that prevents them from spreading the Bharati cult,' and argued that 'the agitation for making Bharati's works common property has been started not from an intellectual and moral point of view' but was 'founded on a thoroughly wrong notion that I have been making fabulously large profits out of the sales'.

Visvanathan also observed, quite rightly: 'The question of nationalisation of the sales of the works of a poet or author is raised in no other part of India.' He asked, 'Do not people consider it as quite natural that the works of Tagore or Sarojini Devi ... should be published by the author or his or her heirs, legal representatives, assigns or the publishers to whom the works might have been sold?'

Visvanathan's statement not only gives a coherent account of the publishing history but also, in its own way, minces no words in setting out how he came to accede to the state takeover of copyright. Based on his experience of publishing Bharati's works for over a quarter of a century, Visvanathan also gave his views and suggestions on how the government should carry forward the publication of Bharati. Despite having ambiguous feelings about how the nationalization took place, he deserves credit for gifting the prized Bharati manuscripts in his possession. He responded with alacrity whenever the government asked for either information or opinion relating to publishing Bharati. Finally, he made an important contribution to the authorized version that the government attempted after the nationalization.

Transfer of Manuscripts

Visvanathan wanted some changes to be made in the draft deed outlining the manuscript handover which had been proposed by the government. Since the gift was voluntary, a token of his good intentions, he argued that the gift need not be included in the deed; he felt that clauses pertaining to the transfer of the copyright alone would suffice.

He also did not agree with the government's position that made the execution of the deed contingent upon the handing over of the manuscripts. He reminded the government of his conversation with the education minister when he had asked for two months' time to ferret out the manuscripts from his home, the office of Bharati Prachuralayam and other places, and to consolidate and list them. He reiterated that there was no change in his commitment to gifting the manuscripts. 'My offer once made is always there and I will carry it out immediately I am free from present pressure of work.' But if in making this gift he had to pay stamp duty, he stated that he would not agree to it.

Regarding the transfer of the consideration owed to him, he wanted Rs 10,000 in the form of national savings certificates and the remaining Rs 5000 as a cheque drawn on the Imperial Bank. These points were made in his letter sent from Manamadurai on 11 April 1949, two months after the nationalization announcement.

In its reply a month later, the government was insistent that the gift of the manuscripts be integral to the deed. However, the government agreed to waive the stamp duty on the gift. Regarding the remittance of the money, it did not accede to Visvanathan's demands and blandly stated that he would be paid in cash at the government treasury.

On 12 May Visvanathan wrote to the government that he had consolidated the manuscripts and was ready to hand them over. He also set out for Chennai to execute the deed. The deed was duly signed on 13 June 1949 at the sub-registrar's office in Mylapore. The education secretary signed on behalf of the government.

Preserving the Manuscripts

As promised, Visvanathan delivered the manuscripts to the education minister with a covering letter dated 14 May 1949. In it he requested the government 'to take necessary measures to preserve them in the Government Museum in a manner worthy of such a national treasure'.

The manuscripts handed over included some 450 pages in the form of notebooks and loose sheets, and included the poet's handwritten texts of *Kuyil*, the Bhagavad Gita (translation), *Panchali Sabatham* and *Chandrikaiyin Kathai*, among others.

Soon the question arose as to how the manuscripts were to be preserved. Shortly after the handover of the manuscripts to the museum, a news item appeared in *The Hindu* (19 August 1949) that the museum proposed to photograph all the manuscripts and exhibit them for the general public as well as to assist the publication of Bharati's works. The news report also noted that since the paper was of very poor quality and would not last if handled freely or kept exposed in a show, there was a proposal to have the manuscripts hermetically sealed in airtight containers.

The Hindu's report caught the attention of Bantwal Surendranath Baliga (1908–58), the distinguished curator of the Madras Record Office (now the Tamilnadu

Archives, one of Asia's largest public archives). Baliga had a PhD in History from the University of London, and became a curator of the government archives at the age of twenty-six. During World War II, when Chennai was being evacuated for fear of Japanese air raids, he oversaw the successful transfer of all the records to Chittoor. His two-volume *Studies in Madras Administration* and the various district gazetteers he produced continue to be useful reference volumes.

Baliga immediately wrote to the education secretary, Lobo Prabhu. The curator was alarmed by the proposal to use airtight containers to seal the manuscripts. Stating that this was 'not the proper method of preserving valuable manuscripts', he drew attention to the likelihood of the papers being damaged either for lack of light and ventilation or through the ravages of insects. He suggested instead the use of methods employed by the British Museum and the Public Record Office of Britain (now the National Archives, Kew) – mending the papers with chiffon and rebinding them with green art canvas covers. In this manner, the manuscripts could be safely exhibited and they could also be handled without fear of damaging them. He offered to mend the manuscripts in the Madras Record Office. Baliga hesitated to make this suggestion to the museum as it was not under his charge and he feared a possible turf war. Baliga explained that he addressed his mail to the education secretary considering the value of the manuscripts and the likelihood of complaints from both the scholarly community and the public at large if any harm were to befall them.

Following this suo moto suggestion, Baliga was instructed by the education secretary to visit the government museum and report on the state of the manuscripts. Baliga reported that the manuscripts were:

> In the shape of exercise notebooks, a dozen in number, each book containing about 40 pages. The writing is in various kinds of ink: black, blue and red. It is clear in some, while it is not so clear in others. The quality of paper is generally very poor. Some of the sheets are brittle and almost all of them require reconditioning.

The superintendent of the government museum at that time was the distinguished anthropologist Ayinapalli Aiyappan. Baliga took Aiyappan to his office and demonstrated the mending process. Baliga also displayed some samples of reconditioned volumes of the East India Company records. Aiyappan was convinced but wanted express permission from the government considering that the 'manuscripts have a sentimental value'. He was understandably wary since he was not a Tamil person.

Baliga collected more details from Aiyappan and reckoned that only about sixty yards of chiffon would be required. He assured the government that he would entrust the work only to expert hands, and that 'every precaution will also be taken to see that none of the manuscripts is damaged in any way in the process of mending'.

As photographing the manuscripts was top priority for Aiyappan, Baliga offered to repair the sheets in each notebook and send them in sections to be photographed. The sheets would be bound once they had been photographed. Baliga also assured that the original covers of the notebooks would be preserved. The binder in his office, Baliga did not forget to add, was 'a man of considerable experience'.

But the government did not want to take any chances. It wrote to Visvanathan asking him if he saw 'any objection, sentimental or other, to the reconditioning of the manuscripts'. Visvanathan replied that he was 'only anxious that [the manuscripts] should be preserved in a manner befitting such a treasure'.

The government approved the proposal to recondition and preserve the Bharati manuscripts. The mended manuscripts are now on display in the government museum at Chennai.

Clearing the Stock

Visvanathan had been constantly publishing Bharati's books over a quarter of a century since the 1920s. He had produced, in various forms, over thirty titles and had kept them almost continuously in print. The decision of the government to take over the copyright, despite the year-long agitation, was made almost overnight. In transferring the copyright, Visvanathan was, of course, alienating his rights and could not legally continue to either publish or sell the books.

Bharati Prachuralayam had a considerable leftover stock at the time of the nationalization. At least thirty-two titles were in print, and the total copies ran into thousands. Visvanathan, in executing the deed, had retained the right to sell not only the leftover stock but also the copies ordered to be printed before the date of the nationalization for a period of a year, that is, until March 1950. The government had given him the licence to do so as it was not only fair but also because it would take considerable time to reprint the books anew, especially for a bureaucratic behemoth like the government. It was agreed that the government would take over the remaining stock if it was not cleared within the licence period.

As the year elapsed, Visvanathan found that he was

still burdened with a considerable part of the stock, especially of the books that had gone for print at the time of the takeover. He therefore requested the extension of the licence to sell the books for a further period of six months, that is, until the end of September 1950. He also requested that the government issue a circular recommending the prescription of the books by schools and their purchase by libraries.

The government responded in typical bureaucratic fashion. It asked for the details of sales after the execution of the transfer deed and the volume of stock remaining. It also wanted to know 'what steps you took to dispose of the books within the stipulated period'. Visvanathan swiftly responded that he was following the same methods he had followed earlier and had in fact 'strengthened my establishment in my place of business with a view to expedite the sales', resulting in their 'appreciable' increase.

The government did not show the same alacrity in replying. Visvanathan had to remind the education secretary that 'the continuance or otherwise of my business depends on the nature of [your] reply'. The fear of taking over the unsold stock and the burden of disposing it of weighed on the government's mind, and, not surprisingly, the licence was extended for another six months.

But there was still much unsold stock left on 30 September 1950, and the government took over the stock for a sum of Rs 15,729 after a discount of 30 per cent on the cover price. The stock was moved to the Government Press Publications branch on the arterial Mount Road for sale to the public. Public announcements of the availability of the books were said to have been made, and copies were sold from there.

'The Authorized Version'

Public pressure, lobbying by cultural personalities and the commitment of some of the cabinet members to Bharati had led to the nationalization of the poet's works. Even though the state had made a public commitment to make Bharati 'available for the use of the public generally at as cheap a cost as possible' and 'make arrangements as they think fit', it was only a pious wish expressed in governmentalese with no mechanism for realizing this vision. The elaborate discussion in the government files leading up to the decision shows no awareness of how the state would deal with the matter once it had taken over the copyright.

Visvanathan's long statement did deal with this issue, and yet as someone who discussed the matter at length with the education minister and the officials, he too did not seem to have clarity on this. He prefaced his suggestions with: 'A great responsibility has now fallen on the shoulders of the Government. Among other things the spirit of the transaction is that they must make the works available to the public at as low a price as possible.' To achieve this, in his view, two courses were open to the government:

(i) To undertake the publications themselves by setting up a proper machinery competent to increase the variety of the editions (such as illustrated prize and library editions), translate the works and compile such extracts as may be fit for introduction as text-books in schools. Here is an opportunity for the Government not only to serve the public but also to popularize the works of the poet beyond the limits of the province. (ii) As an alternative they might authorize some publishers to bring out the works on the lines that may be suggested and on conditions that may be laid down by the Government to ensure cheapness and decent get-up.

Later, as the time for clearing the stock was being discussed, even though he had stated, 'I have all along been avoiding the limelight and will continue to do so, particularly after I have ceased my connection with the publications of the works of Bharati. I shall remain content with having done some service to the poet,' he could not so easily give up his long association. If the government intended to appoint separate agents to print and publish the books, he requested that he too may be appointed as one such agent.

This suggestion indicates that Visvanathan thought the government might adopt a system of appointing authorized agents to license publication and distribution. He made this request on the grounds of his long experience. Alternatively, if the government decided to publish on its own and were to set up an editorial committee for this purpose, Visvanathan said that he was prepared to serve on it given that he had traced, collated, edited and published Bharati for many decades.

It was the second alternative that the government considered. After acquiring the copyright, the government retained its monopoly over Bharati's works.

~

It was the undeclared policy of the government to publish an authorized version of Bharati's works. Towards this end, the DPI, in late October 1950, constituted a Bharati Works Publication Committee consisting of Kalki R. Krishnamurthy, the nationalist writer of great popularity; K. Swaminathan, professor of English, principal of a government college, and later the editor of the monumental *Collected Works of Mahatma Gandhi*; the by-now-familiar Visvanathan; and R.P. Sethu Pillai, professor of Tamil at the University of Madras. Apart from Visvanathan, only Kalki could claim any proficiency in Bharati and his works. Swaminathan, Sethu Pillai, and the later nominees to the committee – Dr M. Varadarajan, celebrated author and professor of Tamil, and K.V. Jagannathan, the last student of the great Tamil scholar-editor U.V. Swaminatha Iyer and editor of the Tamil monthly *Kalaimagal,* were included in the committee on the grounds of their scholarly standing. In fact, some activists of the Bharati Viduthalai Kazhagam expressed their displeasure at these nominations. Narana Duraikannan wondered why people who had no part to play in the campaign for liberating Bharati, and had even been actively hostile to the demand, were nominated to the committee.

The first meeting of the committee was held on 9 December 1950, nearly two years after the government had taken over the copyright. The first issue that confronted the committee was the unsold stock taken over from Visvanathan two months ago. From the stock of the collected volumes of Bharati – one of poetry and two of prose – it was found that only eighteen, fifteen and fourteen copies respectively had been sold by the government over a period of four months from April

1951. This was no index of Bharati's popularity but only a reflection of the government agency's utter inefficiency.

The committee was wise enough to understand this. It therefore suggested that the best way to dispose of the stock was to give it for distribution to well-known and reputed booksellers such as Swadesamitran Puthagasalai, Saiva Siddhanta Works Publishing Society, Tamil Pannai, Kalaimagal Kariyalayam, E.M. Gopalakrishna Kone (of Madurai) and Palaniappa Bros. (of Tiruchirappalli). Since Visvanathan had handed over the stock at a discount of 30 per cent, the committee recommended that the above distributors be offered 25 per cent discount on the cover price.

The government did not take a positive view of this recommendation, and the stock was handed over to the DPI, and as mentioned earlier, it was kept for sale in the department office of Government Press Publications on Mount Road.

The government was flooded with enquiries from various publishers requesting permission to publish, translate and broadcast Bharati's works. Companies such as The Gramophone Co. Ltd (HMV) and AIR pestered the government with demands to record and broadcast Bharati's songs. HMV demanded that as their 'desire [was] to popularize' Bharati's songs, they should be given permission, also pointing out that they had earlier acquired Meiyappan's permission for specific songs. G.T. Sastri, director of AIR, Chennai station, argued that since Meiyappan had given free permission, the government too should continue the practice.

These demands and requests were made within days of the government's announcement of the takeover of Bharati's copyright. While the government had no hesitation in letting AIR, a public company, continue free use of the songs, it was undecided about demands from others. This was symptomatic of the government's inexperience and bureaucratic attitude in handling copyright issues. Since there was a delay in the actual execution of the deed of absolute gift, it was decided that until the deed was signed the rights would continue to vest with Meiyappan. Avinashilingam was also not sure of the date from when Meiyappan would convey the rights but hoped it would be from the date of consent (12 March 1949) rather than the date of the signing of the deed. Meiyappan agreed to the earlier date.

The government had a tough time handling publication requests as the amount involved for the use of Bharati's works was small, and maintaining records and monitoring permissions was cumbersome. When it came to translation, the government was not sure about the subsidiary rights.

The government earned displeasure rather than credit

in the years immediately following the nationalization, until the entire works were put in the public domain.

On the recommendation of the Bharati Works Publication Committee, the government declared that nominal fees for permissions would be charged, and the following were the official rates: (i) Payment of Rs 5 for 250 words subject to a minimum of Rs 5 from an author or a publisher wishing to include passages in any textbook, (ii) Payment of Rs 200 from the producer of any film for the use of a song, (iii) Royalty of 2.5 per cent on the sale price of gramophone records.

Soon the task of granting permissions became onerous for a committee that met at best once in three months. After handling permission requests for about a year, the committee suggested that publication requests be discharged by the DPI. The committee must have also felt that producing an authorized version, rather than approving and passing files, was its primary duty. However, the committee wanted to retain the power of granting requests for films and gramophone recordings.

The large number of files relating to permission requests testifies to the immense popularity of Bharati's poems and the huge demand to use them. But this also opened the sluice gates for the charge that Bharati who was once imprisoned by private individuals was now in the stranglehold of the government. The strict government procedures regarding trade discount to booksellers caused considerable heartburn. In a society that did not value IPRs, many were, not surprisingly, averse to shelling out money for the use of what after all was a mere cluster of words. Bharati enthusiasts fumed at the government's handling of copyright permissions, distribution methods and, more importantly, the delay in producing new editions, whether authorized or not.

As the leading Bharati scholar of the time R.A. Padmanabhan observed, 'For many years, due to bureaucratic red tape, the public suffered, unable to figure out whether the books were available or not. Even those who were aware of the availability found it well-nigh impossible to procure it if they happened to live outside Chennai.'

~

As the stocks slowly dwindled – despite the indolence of the government's publications division's sales machinery – and as many of Bharati's books went out of stock, the pressure on the Bharati Works Publication Committee mounted.

In the meeting of the committee convened in Kalki's home on 30 June 1951, a resolution was passed to the effect that it was 'urgently necessary' to produce the complete works in six volumes. It also recommended the constitution of a subcommittee consisting of R.P. Sethu Pillai, Parali S. Nellaiyappa Pillai, M. Varadarajan and K.V. Jagannathan to curate and edit Bharati's writings for publication. It requested the government to provide the necessary support especially in terms of staff to execute the task. It also suggested that the printing work be executed in a private press rather than in the government press. In order to push the sale of unsold stock, it suggested that the government advertise in dailies and weeklies of the ready availability of Bharati's books.

In response, the DPI felt that 'sales is not encouraging' due to the fact that the available stock was in the form of collected volumes and not individual works, which were 'cheap and easily saleable'. It did not agree with the committee's suggestion to approach private presses.

Disappointed with the slow response of the government, the committee, in its meeting of 11 February 1952, reminded the government of its resolutions passed eight months earlier. Meanwhile, the subcommittee had met several times and edited the poems, and they were ready to go to press. The government asked the committee to justify the demand for an editorial subcommittee and the need to resort to a private press.

Given the government's response, the committee said it was willing to use the government press but had hesitated only because the press was overworked. The committee said that as long as the government press executed the work promptly and neatly, there could be no objection. The committee also clarified that it did not require separate funds or permanent staff but only the permission to incur incidental expenses for clerical assistance, proofing, etc. It reiterated that early steps for re-editing and printing of the poems be given priority. It justified the need for an editorial subcommittee because of the public feeling that the best expert opinion should be solicited.

Finally, the committee met the education secretary on 9 June 1952, more than a year and a half after its constitution. It was agreed that the publication of the poetical works would get top priority; that the printing would be executed in the government press; and that there would be two types of publications: a single-volume library edition printed on high-quality paper and 'attractive get-up', and a four-volume edition on cheaper paper, both with a print run of 1000 copies each. The committee also desired to reclassify the poems, with a different selection and rearrangement, and add a life sketch of the poet and his photograph to every volume. Visvanathan was to prepare the press copy with the necessary introduction, appendices and notes. Editing

Nationalization and After

and proofing was to be carried out by M. Varadarajan and K.V. Jagannathan.

By the end of 1952 the committee was dissatisfied with the earlier decision on the print run. It now wanted to print 3000 copies, justifying the increase on two grounds: that this would help to reduce the price; moreover, as the poems had been out of print for a long time the demand was likely to be 'vigorous'.

As this process was on, pressure was mounting. There were few avenues to meet the increased demand. In the complaints and suggestions book kept in the sales depot of the government press, many voiced their concern. The situation was so grave that many began to wonder if the decision to nationalize Bharati had been an ill-advised move.

Meanwhile, several political changes had taken place. As a result of intra-party factional struggles, Ramaswamy Reddiar, who had authorized the nationalization, had to resign from his premiership within two months of the nationalization. P.S. Kumaraswamy Raja succeeded him. With India adopting a new constitution and becoming a sovereign republic on 26 January 1950, Madras province became Madras state, and Kumaraswamy Raja continued in office but now as chief minister. In the first general elections in early 1952, the Congress party failed to win a majority, and Rajaji became chief minister. Avinashilingam had become a member of parliament and was no more the education minister of the state. Amidst these changes, there was no political leader who cared whether Bharati was in print or not.

There was all-round resentment. One lay Bharati enthusiast, an Iyengar Brahmin from Srirangam, wrote a personal mail to Rajaji in a colloquial language straight from his heart, lamenting the non-availability of Bharati's books. The chief minister was startled by this state of affairs. 'What is the exact position about Bharati's works now?' he queried the education secretary. 'I am wholly ignorant. I would like to have a brief and accurate note.' On receipt of a detailed note that set out the background and the developments since the nationalization of the copyright, he asked: 'Who is in actual charge of revision and printing in connection with the bringing out of the new authorized government edition?' He also asked that this be done soon and the books be supplied to all libraries at cost.

The new education minister C. Subramaniam concurred. But this was nearly a year after the chief minister had asked for the report. 'I was hoping that these new editions would become available at least by this year's Bharathi Day, i.e. 11th September [1953]', but confessed that 'it looks like it will not be possible'.

Nationalization and After

It was finally in May 1954 that the controller of stationery and printing wrote that the complete run of the library edition of poetical works had been printed and was being bound. But he added a caveat: 'it will take a considerable time for printing in gold letters on the spine', and added for good measure that it would take more than a month and a half for the supplies to reach the sales depot. To rub it in, the library edition was to be priced at an exorbitant seven and a half rupees a copy.

By this time Rajaji's so-called Modified Scheme of Elementary Education, pushed through by the chief minister, had run into rough weather. Periyar and Annadurai ran a campaign that the scheme was a blatant attempt to reinforce hereditary caste-based occupations. Rajaji lost the confidence of his party's legislators and was forced to resign. K. Kamaraj became the new chief minister.

Between the declaration of the nationalization and the actual publication of the authorized edition, Tamilnadu had seen four heads of government.

Neither the speed with which the books were being published nor the price satisfied the reading public and Bharati enthusiasts. The press carried reports and news items on mounting displeasure. The popular expectation of easy availability having been belied, a journal from Coimbatore wrote in exasperation: 'Even after four years since [the nationalization] there is little sign of our expectations being fulfilled. Let alone cheap editions, even ordinary editions are not to be had. Given the government's apathy the situation is slipping to a state where one is forced to cry out, "Even if you can't be of assistance, at least leave things alone!'" If the government was overburdened with other administrative work, the journal helpfully suggested, an agency like the Tamil Academy may be given a grant and entrusted with the task of publishing affordable editions.

Jeevanandam, who was now a member of the state legislature, reflected this popular mood in the house. In a starred question, he reminded the government that the raison d'être of the nationalization was the ready and easy availability of Bharati's books at a reasonable price, but the manner in which it was being executed was far from the professed ideal. The education minister could only give a defensive answer: 'The intention of the Government is to have a publication properly edited so that the correct version of the poet may be made available to the public.' More significantly, he added: 'After that anybody is free to publish his works.' In stating this the government was only reiterating the chief minister's statement on the floor of the house in March 1954: 'Once a correct text of the work was made available from the Govt. Press private publishers may compete with one another in producing them as cheaply and as widely as possible' – an assurance that the finance minister too had given a few months later.

Finally, on 14 March 1955 – almost six years after the announcement to nationalize Bharati – following a consultative meeting with the Bharati Works Publication Committee, C. Subramaniam announced to the house:

> Bharatiar's works were held almost as private property and ... nobody could use them for any purpose without the permission of those individual owners. Therefore, in order to make them a public property, the Government purchased the entire right of publishing Bharatiar's works. The intention of the Government then was to publish an authoritative version of the work of Bharati and then release them to the public so that they might be utilized to the best advantage possible. In spite of very many efforts made by the committee constituted for this purpose, it has been so far possible only to publish the poems ... As far as the poems are concerned, the Government have taken a decision to release the entire right to the public. The only restriction with regard to the use of these poems is that in publishing them and in using them in various other ways the public should stick to the authorized version and should not make a variation ... the Government are proposing to issue a

Government Order immediately releasing the entire right to the public so much so Bharatiar's poetical works imprisoned in the hands of private individuals and subsequently within the four walls of the Secretariat will hereafter be completely released and will have complete freedom... Hereafter the cry that Bharatiar's works are not available in any of the bookshops will not be made. I am sure the spirit of Bharati will pervade the entire Tamilnadu and will be infused into our children – our young boys and girls – and that they will live up to the ideals put forward by poet Bharati.

Looking closely at the deliberations in the government files, it appears that even after the publication of the so-called authorized version, most officials felt that the copyright should continue to vest in the government and that a permission fee (erroneously referred to as royalty) should be levied on its use by publishers and others. Some suggested that the government could wait until the then imminent passing of the new Indian Copyright Act (1957). It is clear that the elected government, especially Kamaraj and C. Subramaniam, were convinced that this grated against the popular mood, and vetoed such bureaucratic suggestions.

Not only did the government finally put the poetical works in the public domain but also wisely decided against reprinting their authorized editions as private publishers made a beeline to publish the books. This decision was duly communicated to the committee.

But the government did not devise any mechanism to ensure that publishers followed the authorized edition. Visvanathan had alerted the government on this issue soon after assigning his copyright.

> There is also another danger which the Government must try to avoid. When fresh editions are brought out, care must be taken to see that original lines or stanzas are not tampered with. There is already a tendency to replace some lines or words in the original by those that will suit or [are] liked by the singer, citer or publisher, according to his need and persuasion. There is also a movement to clip, touch up and give a different reading to some of the classics in the name of interpolations and later accretions. Whatever may be the justification for such a process in the case of other writers, there is no room for such a thing in the case of Bharati.

This would fall within the domain of moral rights, and legally it is not clear in whom such rights would subsist – the state of Tamilnadu or Bharati's family. In an infantile book market this was perhaps too complicated a question to deal with.

Who Owns That Song?

In this situation, the convener of the committee, Kalki, died suddenly and prematurely in December 1954. As a number of editorial issues needed to be sorted out, the reconstitution of the committee was inevitable. While the DPI, as could be expected, recommended a respected academic, M. Varadarajan, for the position, C. Subramaniam, in consultation with the other committee members, thought it fit to nominate M.P. Periyasamy Thooran, who, though only a schoolteacher, was at that time the chief editor of Avinashilingam's dream project, the Tamil encyclopedia. More than twenty years ago, Thooran, as a young man of barely twenty, had walked into the office of *Swadesamitran* and, with youthful audacity, asked for permission to consult its back volumes so that Bharati's writings could be culled from it. In 1954 he would publish these gleanings with chronological notes in a landmark edition titled *Bharati Tamil*. Thooran was, therefore, an appropriate choice. And so, C. Subramaniam offered Varadarajan membership in the committee.

In order to underline the primary function of the committee, it was rechristened the Bharati Works Publication Advisory Committee.

Once the authorized edition of the poems was published, the committee diverted its attention to Bharati's prose. But the 'urgency' shown in publishing the poems was missing in this venture. Bharati was seen primarily as an inspired and game-changing poet. Though his prose is no less, it did not evoke the same passion. While the poems were published in 1954, his stories and the first volume of essays took another five years to be published (1959). The subsequent two volumes of essays were published in 1961 and 1963 respectively. The clamour of complaints that marked the delay in publishing the poetical works did not plague the committee as it slowly churned out the prose volumes.

While this is not the place to evaluate the quality of the authorized versions, a few comments are in order. While the authorized edition was modelled on the earlier Bharati Prachuralayam editions, the classification adopted became fixed with scores of publishers reprinting them. When Sakthi Karyalayam produced its edition in 1957 and sold 15,000 copies in a month, the compilation format was easily duplicated by other publishers. Some newly discovered songs were added in the Sakthi edition and figured as an addendum under the rubric 'Some New Songs'. Sixty years later, most editions continue to retain this rubric. Newly discovered songs identified by Bharati experts remain in scholarly monographs and editions, and are unable to find their way into the popular editions.

Though Bharati used few Sanskrit words in his poems, in keeping with the times he employed a significant number of Sanskrit words in their titles. By the time of the authorized version, language politics had changed so much that the committee Tamilized the titles. While this undoubtedly aided the widespread diffusion of the poems, it confused the scholarly community.

The publication committee relied on first editions, Bharati Prachuralayam editions and, to a limited extent, on the manuscripts gifted by Visvanathan to arrive at its reading. Even though the help of experienced scholar-editors such as Vaiyapuri Pillai and K.V. Jagannathan, and the venerated poet S. Desigavinayagam Pillai was sought, the committee did not follow rigorous methods of textual criticism. Nor did it try to trace the journals in which many of the poems were first published. That said, it should be remembered that it was still early days and such methods were not considered appropriate for what was only a contemporary text. Further, for the committee members who carried out this challenging editorial task, it was not a full-time job. Given the constraints under which the committee functioned, their edition, even if it did not measure up to an authorized version, was nevertheless a commendable job.

With its publication, a decade-and-a-half-long struggle came to an end. The initial fervour of demands, the righteous tone in which they were articulated and the protracted route that the nationalization took make it a unique story in literary history.

Epilogue

'More Freely than Kerosene and Matchboxes'

What began as an obscure resolution in a writers' conference caught fire with the filing of a copyright infringement suit and set off a train of events leading to the nationalization of Bharati's writings. It was a drama that involved some of the most interesting personalities of twentieth-century India.

The Navajivan Trust held the copyright of Gandhi until it lapsed and his writings passed into the public domain in January 2009. Nehru's copyright will vest in Sonia Gandhi until the end of 2024. Under the then operative Copyright Act, Tagore's copyright should have been freed from the stranglehold of Visva-Bharati in 1992. P.V. Narasimha Rao's minority Congress government enacted an ordinance to extend Tagore's copyright by another ten years, and Tagore's works came into the public domain only in 2002. The status of Ambedkar's copyright remained unclear (regarding whether the Maharashtra government was the sole custodian of the copyright), and was resolved only in January 2017, with the lapse of sixty calendar years from his death.

Against such a backdrop, the Bharati story is indeed unique.

At a time when a market for books was non-existent, poetry was Bharati's occupation. He died prematurely in impecunious circumstances. His family failed to capitalize on his writings and, in what can be termed as distress sale, the copyright changed hands. It ultimately passed on to someone who was a family member, the poet's half-brother. Even then, it only came into his hands through a commercial transaction, and not as family property.

The market value of Bharati's writings increased in the context of an ascendant Indian nationalist movement and Tamil cultural awakening. The advent of broadcast technology with gramophone and radio and the exponential popularity of talkies immensely added to the commercial value of his songs. Cultural patrimony transformed into material wealth. A copyright infringement notice issued by a film producer triggered a process culminating in the state takeover of Bharati. The leaders of a newly independent state, raised on

'More Freely than Kerosene and Matchboxes'

Bharati's songs, could not possibly endorse restrictions on their use and, therefore, yielded to the demand for their nationalization. In a move without precedent, the state takeover of Bharati's copyright involved considerable legal complexities, which the Madras government, especially its education minister, handled deftly.

If the copyright had not been alienated and had remained with the family, would the demand for nationalization have succeeded, if at all it could have even been raised? Unlikely. The demand gained moral force only because the copyright holders made considerable financial profits while the poet's wife and daughters lived in dire straits; although, ironically, nobody cared about Bharati's wife and daughters, till the very end, when they had to appeal for some compensation.

What was the tangible outcome of nationalizing Bharati? Despite the long delay in producing a so-called authorized version of Bharati's works, the government's editions served as a template. This was later adopted by private publishers, greatly easing their work and making the editions fairly reliable. That Bharati's poems sold in tens of thousands, in an as yet undeveloped book market, was no mean achievement. The total copies printed over the past half a century could possibly exceed a few million. A 500-page book of Bharati's poems can be bought for less than a hundred rupees today – an achievement that could not have been matched by the most resourceful publisher.

The nationalization of Bharati's works has also had other positive consequences. Freedom from copyright enabled many Bharati scholars to ferret out his uncollected writings and produce many volumes, with different kinds of editions made available.

In the field of performing arts and in cinema, Bharati has not been guarded by a jack-in-office like Visva-Bharati. Artists have had the creative liberty to musically build upon his songs. Tamil cinema has extensively used Bharati's songs, making many of them greatly popular.

In the early years of this millennium, the descendants of Thangammal sought to reopen the question of the nationalization of Bharati's works. Thangammal's daughter, the poet's granddaughter, S. Vijaya Bharati, wondered how the government took over the copyright, and raised questions such as who received the compensation and whether the amount was fair. She charged that all sound recordings made thus far of Bharati's songs amounted to piracy. She also alleged that all publishers have exploited Bharati's writings for mercenary interests. Vijaya Bharati's daughter, Mira T. Sundara Rajan, claimed that Visvanathan had signed 'under financial duress', that the nationalization has resulted in 'pseudo-scholarship' and that publishers'

'More Freely than Kerosene and Matchboxes'

profits could run into 'multi-millions of rupees'. She also argued that Bharati's moral rights had been consistently violated. While a case may be made for the infringement of moral rights, the other contentions cannot be substantiated by facts. In any case, there is no way the clock can be turned back.

Forty years after Bharati's works were taken over by the government, his disciple Bharatidasan's writings were nationalized in 1990, twenty-six years after his death. This was followed by the nationalization of the works of Pattukkottai Kalyanasundaram, a communist songster. In 1995, in a fit of competitive claim over the legacy of the Dravidian Movement, Chief Minister J. Jayalalithaa nationalized C.N. Annadurai's writings by paying out a huge sum to his widow. Since the 1990s the government of Tamilnadu has nationalized over a hundred Tamil writers. What was once a unique honour has now been converted into a support scheme for the indigent families of Tamil writers. That is a different story, which does not detract from the momentous saga of Bharati's nationalization.

All said, Bharati's hope that his books would be as 'freely and easily available as kerosene and matchboxes' has not been belied.

A Note on the Sources

Subramania Bharati has been ill-served by biographers in English. A few short biographies of him have been published by the Indian state's cultural agencies such as the Sahitya Akademi and the National Book Trust. His birth centenary (1982) saw the publication of a few more short biographies. N. Subramanian's idiosyncratic and irreverent *Psychobiography of C. Subramania Bharati* (Ennes, 2000) is nevertheless interesting. However, so much exciting new material on Bharati has been unearthed in recent times that these have been rendered dated. This new material remains unsynthesized even in Tamil.

Arguably, the poetry is more important than a poet's life. But Bharati's poetry, unfortunately, does not travel well in English. The cottage industry of translating Bharati has done little to enhance his reputation beyond

A Note on the Sources

Tamil speakers. *Subramania Bharati: Chosen Poems and Prose* (edited by K. Swaminathan, All-India Subramania Bharati Centenary Celebrations Committee, Government of India, 1984) contains a reasonably good selection of his writings. It includes Bharati's prose poems in A.K. Ramanujan's translation. The Sahitya Akademi's two volumes in translation (*Subramania Bharati, Vol. 1: Poems, Vol. 2: Essays and Stories*, edited by Sirpi Balasubramaniam, 2016–17) are only the most recent reminders of the difficulties and challenges in translating Bharati. Earlier translations include those by Prema Nandakumar (Sahitya Akademi, 1978); P.S. Sundaram (Vikas, 1982); J. Parthasarathy (Bharati Tamil Sangam, 1982); Nakulan (Zha, 1982); T.N. Ramachandran (ed., Tamil University, 1989); and Usha Rajagopalan (Everyman, 2012). Arguably, one of the better translations, by M.L. Thangappa, remains uncollected. A few of these translations now form an appendix to this book. Bharati's own writings in English are to be found in *Agni and Other Poems and Translations & Essays and Other Prose Fragments* (1980), but it does not include new material unearthed in the last few decades.

There are a few extended studies in English of Bharati's poetry. K. Kailasapathy's short book *On Bharati* (NCBH, 1986) contains two breezy essays. K. Meenakshisundaram's *A Study of the Achievements of Bharati as a Poet* (1982),

A Note on the Sources

S. Ramakrishnan's *Bharati: Patriot, Poet, Prophet* (NCBH, 1982) and V. Satchidanandan's *Whitman and Bharati* (Macmillan, 1978) are useful.

Many of the above books, apart from being dated, are not in print any more.

My understanding of Bharati, while enriched by existing scholarship, is based on my own reading of his works and the primary research I have conducted in the colonial and other archives. My discoveries include the twenty issues of the daily *Vijaya* that he edited, and his writings in *The Hindu*.

In Tamil, all Bharati scholars are indebted to the pioneering work of P. Thooran and R.A. Padmanabhan. The latter's pictorial biography, *Chitrabharati*, remains a classic. Seeni. Viswanathan's monumental thirteen-volume chronological edition of Bharati's complete works remains indispensable as are his many other compilations and studies on Bharati. Y. Manikandan's recent discoveries greatly refine our knowledge of Bharati.

My understanding of the advent of new broadcast media in the 1920s and 1930s is owed to Stephen P. Hughes, especially his 'The "Music Boom" in Tamil South India: Gramophone, Radio and the Making of Mass Culture', *The Historical Journal of Film, Radio and Television*, 22 (4), 2002.

As for the subject of this book, the only extended

narrative available is Ediroli Viswanathan's *Bharatikku Viduthalai* (Sekar Pathippagam, 1972); a revised version is his *Makkal Pottrum Mahakavi* (Sakthi Pathippagam, 1981). Largely based on file clippings, then in the possession of T.K. Shanmugam (now apparently lost), and interviews with some of the actors in this drama, it provides an uncomplicated but nevertheless rich narrative of 'the liberation of Bharati'.

This and other such narratives draw from a few sources. T.K. Shanmugam's memoir, written on the occasion of his sixtieth birthday, a year before his death: *Enathu Nataka Valkai* (Vanathi Pathippagam, [1972] 1986) and the biography of Omandur P. Ramaswamy Reddiar by Somalay, *Vivasaya Mudhalamaichar* (Vedaranyam Gurukulam, 1979). AV. Meiyappan's self-serving account may be found in his memoir, which was first serialized in the popular Tamil weekly *Kumudham* and subsequently published as *Enathu Valkai Anubhavangal* (AV.M. Aranilayam, [1974] 2000); its English translation is available as *My Experiences in Life* (AVM Charities, 2015). The book includes a facsimile of the deed of absolute gift made by him to the government.

Brief mentions of the controversy may be found in the various short biographies and memoirs of Narana Duraikannan and Vallikannan.

Quite bafflingly, there is but one line in the

autobiography of T.S. Avinashilingam (*The Sacred Touch: An Autobiography*, Avinashilingam University, [1986] 2000) wherein the nationalization of Bharati is listed as one among the many achievements of the Congress ministry. In this instance, at least, one can only regret the otherwise noble trait of modesty and self-effacement.

The full text of P. Jeevanandam's talk at the inauguration of the Bharati Manimantapam at Ettayapuram where he forcefully articulated the demand of nationalization can be found in his *Bharati Vazhi* (NCBH, [1964] 1993).

I have discussed the publishing history of Bharati's works at length in my *The Province of the Book: Scholars, Scribes and Scribblers in Colonial Tamilnadu* (Permanent Black, 2012). For a full treatment of Bharati's engagement with Tagore and his works, see my 'Bharati on Tagore' (*Seminar*, No. 623, July 2011).

As the process of nationalization involved the state from the beginning to the end, I have relied on a wealth of government documents to reconstruct the whole drama. These documents had remained untapped for over half a century. (These files, called Government Orders, housed in the Tamilnadu Archives, Chennai, are numbered and prefixed by the abbreviation G.O.) The cornerstone of my narrative is a bulky document (G.O. No. 2467, Education & Public Health, 2-8-1949) that I was lucky to locate. This file contains, among other documents,

A Note on the Sources

T.K. Shanmugam's representations to the government; the propagandist pamphlet that he distributed; copies of various contracts signed by Chellamma Bharati, C. Visvanathan, AV. Meiyappan, Jeshinglal K. Mehta and others as the various rights changed hands; details of court proceedings; etc. The gradual evolution of government policy on the issue is discernible in the notes in this file written by various officials and ministers.

The payments to the Bharati family on the successful takeover of the copyright are detailed in G.O. No. 963, Education & Public Health, 4-4-1949. Shakuntala Bharati's acceptance of the deal is in G.O. No. 2781, Education & Public Health, 5-9-1949.

The details of the leftover stock of Bharati's books with C. Visvanathan are found in G.O. No. 1226, Education, 17-4-1950. His poignant and informative account of how he came to publish Bharati's works and the circumstances in which he accepted the nationalization, narrated in a cyclostyled statement titled 'Service or Profiteering?', is also in this file. All quotations of C. Visvanathan about the events leading up to the takeover and after are drawn from this rich statement. Additional information on Visvanathan has been drawn from a collection of his articles and interviews on Bharati, *Kavi Pirantha Kathai* (Sri Bhuvaneshwari, 1985).

The section on Mandayam Srinivasacharya's claim over

A Note on the Sources

Bharati's translation of Tagore's stories is based on G.O. No. 3421, Education, 8-11-1949.

The full list and further details on the Bharati manuscripts that C. Visvanathan gifted to the government are in G.O. No. 1534, Education & Public Health, 13-5-1949. The process of preservation of Bharati's manuscripts by the Madras Record Office is detailed in G.O. No. 3788, Education & Public Health, 12-12-1949.

The details of the government-appointed Bharati Works Publication Committee are drawn from G.O. No. 2217, Education, 19-9-1952; G.O. No. 1259, Public (General B), 3-8-1954; G.O. No. 1234, Public (General B), 9-4-1955 and G.O. No. 1399, Public (General B), 18-4-1956. Additional details have been culled from the 'Minutes Book', Bharati Works Publication Committee (Tamil Academy).

The passing of the copyright into the public domain is detailed in G.O. No. 1299, Public (General B), 18-4-1955.

For the views of Thangammal Bharati's descendants, questioning the legality and morality of the nationalization of Bharati's copyright, see S. Vijaya Bharati, 'Bharati Padaippugalil Kappurimai', *Dinamani*, 3 May 2005, and her interview in *Kumudham Dheeranadhi*, April 2004; Mira T. Sundara Rajan, 'Bharati and His Copyright', *The Hindu*, 22-12-2004; 'Moral Rights in the Public

Domain: Copyright Matters in the Works of Indian National Poet C. Subramania Bharati', *Singapore Journal of Legal Studies* (Summer 2001); 'The Lessons of the Past: C. Subramania Bharati and the Nationalisation of Copyright', *Scripted: A Journal of Law, Technology and Society*, 6 (2), 2009.

Full references to all the quotations and other information can be found in my Tamil book *Bharati: Kavignanum Kappurimaiyum* (Kalachuvadu, 2015).

A Note on the Worth of Money

What would the money that C. Visvanathan, and Chellamma Bharati and her daughters received have been worth?

Inflation over a period of seventy years skews our understanding of the relative value of money. Inflation was particularly high during and after World War II, and Madras government employees in fact went on a strike soon after independence demanding higher salaries. Economists use a range of sophisticated methods to calculate the relative worth of money. I have no competence to do so but details below could give broad indicators.

A Note on the Worth of Money

As a rule of thumb, what cost Rs 100 in 1947 would cost Rs 6500 or more at today's prices. 10 gm of gold cost Rs 95 in 1949. In 1951 the average agricultural wages were Rs 20 per month. At the time of independence when salaries for teachers were revised, a trained teacher was fixed on a pay scale of between Rs 70 and Rs 140 per month with an annual increment of Rs 5. An urban middle-class family would have had a monthly income of about Rs 150, spending half of it on food and related items. A cup of coffee could be had for a quarter of a rupee (India Coffee House prices) or less. A popular weekly cost about four annas. A visit to a Chennai cinema would cost from two and a half rupees (the most expensive ticket) to half a rupee for the lowest; seating on the floor was less, at a quarter of a rupee.

The rupee was decimalized in 1957. During the time of the nationalization of Bharati's copyright, 16 annas made a rupee; an anna was 12 paise (192 paise to a rupee). Numerically, it was expressed as, for example, 10–8–3: ten rupees, eight annas and three paise.

Selected Poems of Subramania Bharati

Translated by M.L. Thangappa*

---

* M.L. Thangappa taught Tamil for over twenty-five years and is an accomplished poet and translator. He won the Sahitya Akademi Award for his translation of Tamil Sangam poetry, *Love Stands Alone*.

திரு சிபிரமணிய பாரதி

C. Subrahmania Bharati

The Past Is Past
Sendrathini meelaathu moodare

The past is past, you fools!
It never comes back.
Why cling to its vestiges
And pine for the dead memories
Living in endless hankerings
And fretting yourselves to death?
Let bygones be gone.
Feel intensely
That you are fresh-born
This very day.
Eat and drink
And be merry
Have a song at heart
All your ills
Will wither away.

A Poet's Wishes
Kaani nilam vendum

A tract of land
Mother divine
Let me possess.

And in it, a mansion
With pillars beautiful
And towers shining pure.

A gurgling fountain
To run beside it
Coconut palms around
To give me shade
And tender coconuts.

How would I love here
The pearly splendour of the moon
The cuckoo's crooning notes
And sweet, refreshing breeze.

Give me also
A loving wife
To set my heart ablaze with songs
So that in this bliss of union
Profuse verses flow.

And lastly, Mother,
In this wild expanse around
You must keep me safe
To have this world sustained
By the power of my song.

A Prayer
Manathil uruthi vendum

Grant us firmness of the heart
Give us a pleasing tongue
Let our thoughts be always good
Let us achieve our aims
Make our dreams come true
Let us promptly have our dues
Grant us wealth and pleasure
Greatness without measure.

Let our eyes be opened wide
Make us firm in deed
Free our women from their bonds
God almighty, keep us,
Let us benefit the world
And find heaven on earth
And above all let Truth prevail
Om! Om! Om! All hail!

We Have No Fear
Acchamillai amunkuthalillai

We have no fear, no inhibitions
We do not tremble, feel no shame
We have no sins, no sneakings mean
What e'er befalls disturbs us not,
What of it if oceans surge and swell?
Or the Universe blows up?
We turn not a hair – we pooh-pooh them.
Fear we nothing; fear we none
Fear we nowhere, never, ne'er.
The sky's above us; rains fail not
The sun does shine, the wind blows well
All is well with moon and stars
And with Water, Earth and Fire.
We've 'Body', 'Breath' and 'Intellect'
Riches, women, songs to soothe,
The wondrous world our eyes to please
Lord Ganapathi's name to praise for aye
And so, my heart – all hail to thee! –
Be thou happy! Honest, firm!
Give no room for trickish cares
The 'Flaming God' is our refuge.

The New Russia
Maakaali parasakthi

The Great Mother Kali's merciful glance
Fell on the Russian land, and lo,
There was revolution!
The tyrant fell screaming.
The gods smote their arms in jubilation.
The demons whose tears dried up in fumes of bitterness
Perished in sheer grief.

Like Hiranya the tyrant Tsar had reigned,
Steeped in perdition.
The good and the noble had no refuge,
For the fool had trampled justice under foot
And the land, like a jungle infested with snakes
Became a nest of falsehood, perfidy and vice.

The tillers of the land who toiled and sweated
Were not fed, but with myriad ills beset.
The sycophants who worshipped lies
Enjoyed all the riches while men of truth
Were locked in dungeons of unspeakable atrocities.
Some were hanged; some languished all their life
In that infernal Siberian wilderness.

At the slightest sign of dissent
Prisons awaited men, and protests
Ended in exile. All good was ravaged.
Brutality became law. It was at this hour
The Mother's heart softened. She turned
Her ever-loving eyes on her votaries,
And tyranny came to an end.

The tyrant fell as though the Himalayas fell.
All his coterie who lied and plotted and murdered law
Fell with a mighty crash.
It was like the forest trees suddenly falling
And drying up into a pile of firewood.

The cause of people triumphed, and in a trice
Social justice came to force.
And heralding hope to the world, emerged
A people's democracy.
The fetters of servitude were shattered.
'No more thralldom!' they decreed.
The Demon of the Dark Age fell
Like a crumbled wall.
Let millennium arise!

Acknowledgements

This book originated as an academic paper which received much enthusiasm from scholars and listeners for its fascinating subject matter: 'Really, did the state buy a poet's copyright and make it public?'

Some suggested that it was a shame to reduce this dramatic story to a scholarly article that would be lost in the thick forest of academic journals. I first rewrote and expanded the paper in Tamil keeping the general reader in mind. Readers were not only excited by the drama but also moved by the many poignant moments in the posthumous career of the greatest modern Tamil poet. Kannan Sundaram, my friend, co-conspirator and Tamil publisher, suggested that the book would appeal to English readers as well.

R. Sivapriya, my editor, jumped at the idea when I proposed it to her. In a fit of paroxysmal energy, the manuscript was drafted in a month's time. While keeping

Acknowledgements

to the narrative thread of the original Tamil text, I have introduced the dramatis personae to the non-Tamil reader through interesting details about their lives. The first chapter sets up the story, leading to the drama surrounding the nationalization of Bharati's works.

The book is based on contemporary accounts and memoirs as well as a wealth of government documents. I was especially lucky to locate a bulky file which records the process of the government takeover, in the Tamilnadu Archives in Chennai. For the sake of easy reading, I have not provided notes and references but have instead appended a note on the sources. Interested scholars may refer to my Tamil book (*Bharati: Kavignanum Kappurimaiyum*, Nagercoil: Kalachuvadu Pathippagam, 2015) for a complete set of references.

My thanks are due to the many friends who have helped me in various ways with this book. Special mention needs to be made of P. Athiyaman, Y. Manikandan and B. Mathivanan, friends and scholars, who were my sounding boards. Aditya Balasubramanian and Vikram Raghavan gave the manuscript a critical reading but are exonerated from any blame for the end result.

The book has greatly benefited from Sivapriya's keen eye and experienced hand. Janani Ganesan did a fine job of editing the manuscript with great enthusiasm. Thanks to Shyama Warner for carefully reading the proofs, to

Acknowledgements

Cincy Jose for seeing the book through the press and to Gavin Morris for an excellent cover.

I began my literary career as a fourteen-year-old in what happened to be the centenary year of Bharati's birth, 1981–82. That annus mirabilis has inspired me over the decades as a student of Tamil history, society and culture. I am delighted that I could write this book. Bharati is not nearly as well known as his contemporary Tagore, and I hope this short book will enthuse the reader to find out more about him. And who knows, I might just write a full-length biography of Bharati before his death centenary.

This book is dedicated to Professor V.K. Natraj in acknowledgement of his warmth, generosity and unstinted support of my intellectual career.

Other Books by the Author

As author

- *The Province of the Book: Scholars, Scribes, and Scribblers in Colonial Tamilnadu*
- *In Those Days There Was No Coffee: Writings in Cultural History*

As editor

- *Love Stands Alone: Selections from Tamil Sangam Poetry* (translated by M.L. Thangappa)
- *Red Lilies and Frightened Birds: Muttollayiram* (translated by M.L. Thangappa)
- *In the Tracks of the Mahatma: The Making of a Documentary* (written by A.K. Chettiar)
- *Beyond Tranquebar: Grappling Across Cultural Borders in South India* (with Esther Fihl)
- *Chennai, Not Madras: Perspectives on the City*

As translator

- *J.J.: Some Jottings* (translated by Sundara Ramaswamy)